I TOTALLY MEANT TO DO THAT

I TOTALLY MEANT TO DO THAT

jane borden

BROADWAY PAPERBACKS
NEW YORK

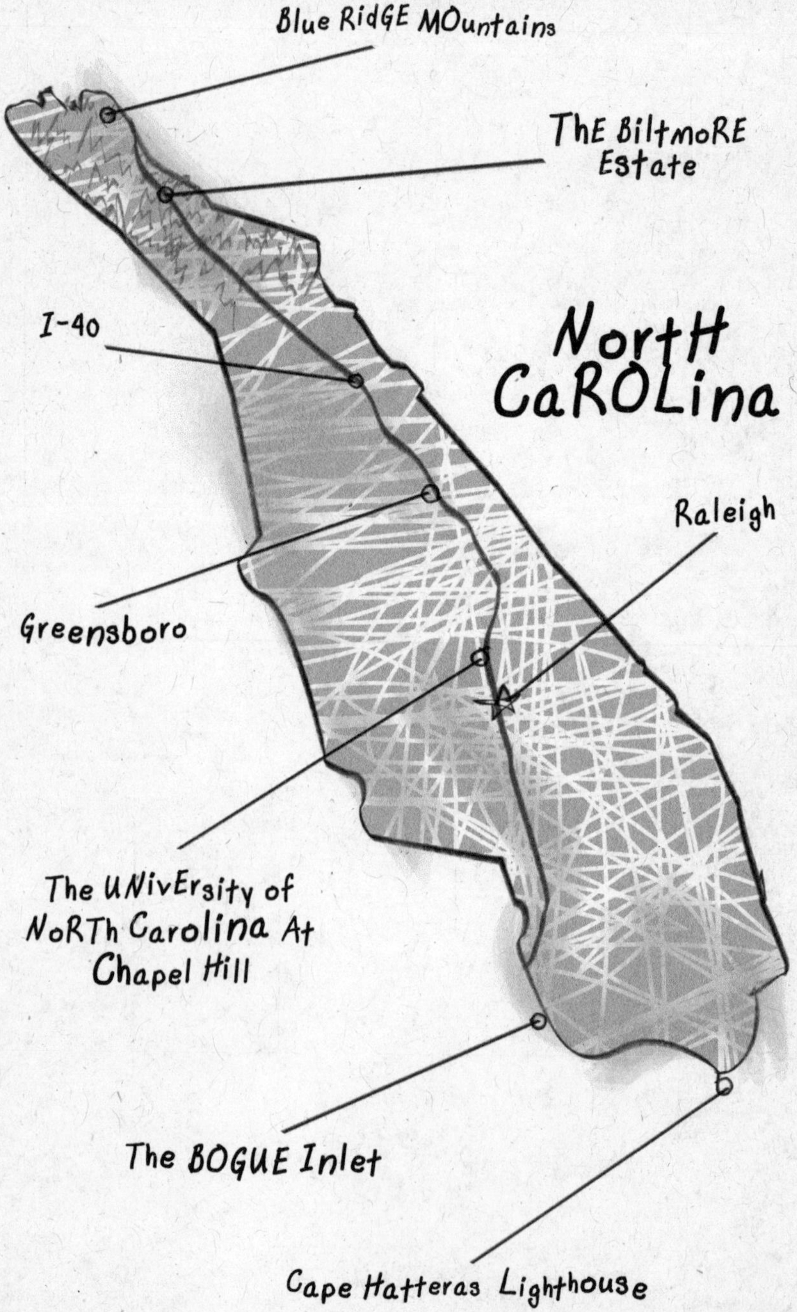

Blue RidGE MOuntains

THE BiltmoRE
Estate

I-40

NortH
CaROLina

Raleigh

Greensboro

The UNivErsity of
NoRTH Carolina At
Chapel Hill

The BOGUE Inlet

Cape Hatteras Lighthouse

Inwood Hill Park, Fort Tryon Park, and Fort Washington Park

ThE CloistErs

MANHATTaN

BroadWAy

The Empire State Building

Central PaRk

The NEW York PuBLic Library

Brooklyn Bridge

The STAtue of Liberty

BROADWAY

Portions or alternative versions of some chapters have been previously published in various magazines: "Dancing with the Enemy" in *The New York Times Magazine;* "Waiting for the Raid Team" in *Time Out New York;* and "Groundhog Day" in *Modern Bride.*

Library of Congress Cataloging-in-Publication Data
Borden, Jane.
    I totally meant to do that/Jane Borden. —1st ed.
        p. cm.
    1. American wit and humor.   I. Title.
    PS3602.O68413 2011
    814'.6—dc22   2010029940

ISBN 978-0-307-46463-7

Printed in the United States of America

Book design by Maria Elias
Map illustrations by Tam Nguyen
Cover design by Misa Erder
Cover illustrations © plainpicture/Lubitz + Dorner
10   9   8   7   6   5   4   3   2

For Nathan

Contents

Prologue: Waiting for the Raid Team

Shu-ku-ku-ku-CLANG!

The last sliver of daylight disappeared as the metal gate shut me inside. I was trapped in one of those squalid knockoff handbag stores in Chinatown, alone, in the dark, and convinced I'd soon have this conversation: "So tell me, Jane, how were *you* sold into the sex-slave industry?" "Well, Svetlana, I tried to buy a fake Prada purse from a Canal Street stall with a Pokémon sheet for a door."

That sheet was now on the other side of a very solid shutter. It click-locked to the ground and my knees went weak. Great: When they found my body, I'd have tee-teed all over my matching denim outfit.

The store, if you can call it that, was no bigger than my minivan and it stunk of fishy noodle soup. I'd probably have to eat the vendor's leftovers to stay alive. I knocked on the barrier and cried, "Hello? What's happ'nin'?" No one answered.

I had come to town to see a Broadway show, eat at Tavern on the Green, and bring back a dozen knockoffs for my girlfriends in Raleigh. I had not come to pursue a career in a Chinese Mafia sweatshop.

There was shouting outside. It had to be the cops. "Let me out of here!" I screamed. "I promise I wuh-int gonna buy nuthin!"

Lord Jesus, I didn't want to go to jail. What would my book club think? What would I tell my husband, the contractor who was currently dove-hunting with the boys at Currituck? Or my twin sister, the one who had the cash for the bags, but couldn't be there today because she'd taken the kids to the Hershey's store in Times Square? Or my bible study leader, who's a closeted homosexual, but...

Wait, why am I lying to you? You're not a counterfeiter. Sorry; old habits die hard.

Here's the truth: I *was* trapped. And I was definitely wearing matching denim, but it was a disguise. I do not own a minivan or a wedding ring. I've never eaten at Tavern on the Green. And I wasn't afraid; I'd been locked inside filthy Canal Street stalls before. It was part of my job description as a spy.

My employer was Holmes Hi-Tech, a private-investigation firm that's now defunct (otherwise I wouldn't write this chapter; I may have been a spy, but I'm no rat). Our clients were Chanel, Louis Vuitton, Rolex, Polo, and other luxury-goods purveyors protecting their trademarks from the sale of illegal knockoffs. New York City's Chinatown is one of the biggest counterfeiting centers in the world. So even though Customs, the police, and the FBI are responsible for busting the illicit trade, a multibillion-dollar industry flourishes regardless, leaving a niche plenty big for our small, spunky Midtown office.

When I first interviewed for the secret-shopper position, and mentioned it to my mother, she forbade me to accept the job. She actually used the word "forbid," a tactic previously unemployed, I suppose, because it had never been necessary. The closest thing to crime rings in Greensboro were the hippie drum circles on the UNC-G campus. And anyway, my parents typically let me make my own mistakes. Although I wish she'd forbidden my eighth-grade perm, going undercover in Chinatown was where she drew the line. Years later, when I confessed to disobeying her, she shot me a look that could have curled hair without chemicals.

Honestly, though, I never felt unsafe in Chinatown; I had anonymity. My boss was the one who received death threats. He was also the one shouting with the vendor outside the Pokémon stall, which I of course knew; I'd been expecting his arrival. Here's how it went down.

A week prior, another of my fellow "spotters" had cased the same location, looking for fake versions of our clients' products. While she fingered purses and scarves, tried on sunglasses, and generally pretended to shop, she was actually memorizing all of the brands being sold, the kinds of items within each brand, in which part of the store each was displayed or behind which secret remote-controlled doors each could be found—multiplied by however many other locations she'd been assigned to visit before she could leave that section of Canal Street and safely purge her brain via pen and paper in a restaurant bathroom. The elderly should pursue this line of work as an exercise to stave off Alzheimer's.

With this intelligence my boss had obtained a warrant to confiscate Pokémon's contraband. He'd surprise the vendor by rolling in with a raid team of off-duty cops and fire fighters. But first, they needed confirmation that the goods remained on-site. Enter me.

By 11:00 a.m. on a Saturday, almost every square foot of Canal

Street, including parts of the road, is occupied by merchandise. Items spill out of stores onto the sidewalk: card tables whose legs splay under the weight of backpacks and wallets, buckets that brim with baby turtles crawling to the top of a mound of themselves. Food carts sell dumplings and noodles curbside. Women wheel jerry-rigged carts stacked with pirated DVDs. Adolescent boys hawk water and soda from coolers on wheelbarrows. Be careful not to trip over one of the dozen or so varieties of motorized toy that flip, flop, slither, and writhe through the squares of municipal concrete just beyond the cash registers that could make them your own. *Invisible* hand of the market? If Adam Smith could wander modern Chinatown, he'd have seen it plain as day. And people call the Chinese communists.

I hit our target, near Baxter on Canal, in my tasteless denim ensemble, around 11:10 and immediately saw what I was after: counterfeit purses. They were on display, so I didn't need to weasel my way through a back room, down a secret staircase, or into a crawl space in the ceiling. It's the little perks that matter.

At that point I acted as if I felt my phone vibrating. When I flipped it open, pretending to answer, I punched the last-number-dialed button.

"Hello?" I said.

Ringing.

"Hey Carol! What's happ'nin'?"

Ringing.

"Not much. I'm shopp—"

"Jane?" answered my manager at Holmes Hi-Tech.

"—ing. Yep."

"Are you at the location?"

"Yes. Dinner tonight; y'all should definitely come!"

"So the bags are there?"

"You got it!"

"Great, I'll send the raid team now."

"No, you're beautiful!" (That last part was just for me.)

I put my phone back in a pocket and moved through the store slowly, regarding every item, taking time so as not to run out of merchandise to inspect. I couldn't leave until the guys arrived; the knockoffs were the evidence my boss took to court, so without them we had no case, and therefore no profession. If Pokémon got spooked for some reason and pulled the illegal bags from the floor, I had to know where he put them, whether in one of the aforementioned hiding spots, or in another location on another block, an outcome I feared, as it would require me to follow, and I was uncomfortable tailing criminals through the streets of Chinatown. I am not a subtle person.

But this vendor wasn't worried about getting busted by a spy. Neither was he concerned about lying to customers. While I modeled scarves, another woman in the stall pointed to a pocketbook without a label and asked, "Is this Gucci?" Without pausing, the merchant answered, "Yes." To trained eyes such as mine or those of a Madison Avenue doyenne, the item in question was clearly patterned after Louis Vuitton. I assumed the vendor was mistaken, until another woman, a few minutes later, grabbed the same purse and asked, "Is this Chanel?" to which he also responded, "Yes." Whatever it takes to make a sale; tell them what they want to hear.

Where the hell was the raid team? It had been almost fifteen minutes. No one spends that much time in a store the size of a minivan unless considering a major purchase, in which case I probably would have approached the salesman by now. But I didn't want to engage him for fear he'd later suspect my involvement, and then, suddenly, oh my God I was the only other person in the store, but, phew, he went outside, and...

Shu-ku-ku-ku-CLANG!

The pleather purses are manufactured for pennies, either in China or in sweatshops, and, obviously, not taxed. Markups can reach eight thousand percent. Salesmen, leases, aliases, and passports are all a dime a dozen; the crooks only cared about the bags—not for their actual worth, but rather their potential, imagined worth. In this never-ending battle, the contraband was our Jerusalem: All sides revolved around it, gained definition from it, and, therefore, assigned it a value far greater than its face.

That's why I was locked inside. Vendors protected their holy crap. They were familiar with raids, so if they saw the team approach—it's hard to miss six beefy mustachioed Irish dudes rolling out of a white van like a clown car of sports announcers—they'd immediately close shop, regardless of patrons inside. Occasionally I was trapped with other confused women, sometimes by myself, but never for long: Warrants trump locks.

When the gates inevitably rose on the other side of the Pokémon sheet—which was, by the way, counterfeit itself—I scurried out like a frightened tourist, careful to avoid eye contact with the guys. I could congratulate them later over beers but couldn't blow my cover at the moment because a couple of days later, I'd be back in Chinatown canvassing the same stretch of junk. My income hinged on my ability to be multiple people. Problem was: I'm not much of an actor.

In the spring of my senior year in high school, I took a season off sports to broaden my artistic horizons. I played Miss Bessom in our theater department's production of Shirley Jackson's adaptation of *The Lottery*. All you need to know about the play is that everyone wears gray and people die, but then again you're probably familiar with the story after seeing *your* high school drama club production. I don't know why this brutally dark play is so popular with adolescents...oh wait, yeah I do.

Anyway, I was horrible. I had a handful of lines and delivered each like a kid who bowls by holding the ball between her legs, and then while squatting, thrusts it down the lane. I am also a bad bowler.

Our director said to smile and project. Apparently I understood that to mean grimace and shout. I'd have been hailed as a star had the stage directions for Miss Bessom read, "played as a man with hearing loss and hemorrhoids." Actually, for my portrayal to have been believable, the description would have needed to read, "played as Jane with hearing loss and hemorrhoids," for I was never actually in character. While the line "I declare, it's been a month of Sundays since I've seen you!" came out of my mouth, running through my head was: "Who talks that way? Why not just say, 'it's been a month'? The Sundays are implied."

The only point in each performance when I felt the slightest association with how Miss Bessom might think and feel was when the Mrs. Dunbar character said to Bessom/me, "They told me you were gettin' real fleshy."

Bottom line: I couldn't act my way out of a paper bag if it were made of me-sized holes. Whatever, no biggie—except that every other spotter at Holmes Hi-Tech was an actor. In fact, it was a thespian friend of mine who'd introduced me to the gig. Actors liked the work because, in addition to the flexible hours, it allowed them to practice their craft. I pursued the job because it sounded cool, the closest to clandestine this suburban girl could get.

I wish I were able to reveal to you a deeper, more complicated motivation—a consuming desire to serve justice, a fascination with Chinese culture, a lurid role-playing fetish. "It sounded cool" is a lame provocation, but there it is nonetheless. I've grown accustomed to the disappointment engendered by that response. People prefer a good story.

My actor coworkers wrote new narratives every morning. After exchanging flyer postcards for various low-budget blackbox-theater one-acts, they'd transform themselves. I remember this brunette who earned the moniker "chameleon." She left the office once as a Canadian-accented tourist and returned that afternoon a Goth teenager, replete with pale makeup and ripped skull-and-crossbones tights. *I* didn't even recognize her.

She was one of only a few who switched from one identity to another beyond the office. Our manager discouraged the practice because there was nowhere safe to do it. She also warned us not to take notes anywhere, not even in a bank or pizza shop, and not to leave information on voice mails within earshot of anyone. She'd lost two spotters that way, one who'd blown his cover in front of an employee at Pearl Paint, and another who'd done so next to an elderly man playing mah-jongg in Columbus Park. Our manager said everyone in Chinatown was involved, "Everyone is in on it." Obviously, that's egregious hyperbole, but I think what she meant to say was that there was no establishment at which we could be certain no one was involved. Indeed, I once happened across a multi-thousand-dollar phony-Rolex deal while hitting the loo at the Lafayette Street Holiday Inn.

The most convincing performers scored the respected roles. One time, during assignments, our manager told this guy Henry that she'd be helping with his disguise that morning. Authenticity was critical, as they needed him to case a location for four straight hours, to monitor who came and went. So Henry became a junkie. He passed the afternoon sitting or standing on the curb, intermittently nodding off. Back at the office, while demonstrating the smackhead lean, wherein the body reaches an angle nearly 45 degrees but some-how, Newton defyingly, does not fall, he explained that he'd deliv-ered a depiction so convincing, it'd attracted the attention of both a cop, who told him he was disorderly and threatened to arrest him, and a born-again Christian, who told him about Jesus and threatened to save his soul.

And then there was I, approaching the disguise closet each time with only this question: Which wig today, the brown one that resembles my actual hair? Or the brown one that's exactly like my actual hair? After the great Miss Bessom debacle, I knew better than to try to act like someone else. Also, I'm a terrible vocal mimic. I can't even ape midwestern, and that's the O-negative blood type of accents: It can flow through anyone. It's the Bill Cosby impression of accents. And I am also bad at those...unless what's been requested is "Bill Cosby doing a Japanese man." So only two characters lived on my résumé. One was me, and the other was a heightened version of me, the me I imagined I'd be if I'd stayed in North Carolina.

Alterna-Me had, for starters, a much thicker drawl, which I could pull off because rather than "doing an accent," I merely tapped into the way I sound when I've had too much to drink. She was young, married, and applying to law schools near her home in Raleigh. She wore pearls and belonged to things like supper clubs and congregations. She grocery shopped at the Harris Teeter and ate lunch on Sundays at the Carolina Country Club. If ever questioned, I could have recited her biography easily. I knew everything about her, even though I am not the one who created her.

"Don't you want to come home and go to law school?" my uncle Lucius used to ask nearly every time we spoke. "Raleigh's nice, you know. It's ranked on the list of most livable cities."

"I'll throw a luncheon for you!" Aunt Jane, for whom I am named, would add, having picked up another phone in the house. "And get you into all the clubs."

"You can join the Episcopal Church."

And then my aunt would shout, "I'll give you all my jewelry!"

So, yeah, this girl was a big part of my life. And somehow, she worked. I canvassed Canal Street three, occasionally four times a week, always wearing a shade of the same person, and got away with it. I didn't need to be a chameleon because the counterfeiters bought *me*. Eventually, I developed a theory regarding why.

Since they knew how we operated, merchants were suspicious of every potential customer, scrutinized each for tells that he or she might be a spy. I noticed them paying special attention to certain people while ignoring others, whomever they could quickly disregard as guileless. I never needed to become a different person, as long as the original was consistently overlooked. And as I've come to understand, people—from, apparently, either hemisphere—assume Southerners are innocent.

It was a wondrous thing to witness. Salesmen eyed me warily until the moment I purred, "Y'all got Gucci?" when they'd instantly drop their guards and either lift a sheet, pull a trash bag from a desk, or open a concealed door in a false wall. It's not as if we were suddenly pals; there were no smiles or secret handshakes. What happened was a dismissal. They dismissed me, shifted mentally from looking at me to looking beyond me, over my shoulder for the next potential threat.

Astute readers would argue that any accent could have put them at ease. And for the most part that's true. Counterfeiters trust tourists. But I'm telling you, there's something foolproof about the drawl. Unlike some of the other spotters, I was almost never denied access. I can only posit that Barney Fife and Elly Mae Clampett exist in the collective unconscious, because I don't think Mao fed his starving republic on a diet of TV Land classics.

Which is to say that maybe it was more than the accent; maybe it was also my accompanying wide eyes and gullible smile. Come to think of it, maybe it was I who worked like a Southern charm.

Once, I asked a peddler if he had "LV" in the store and he whispered, "Not now."

"Why?" I responded vapidly.

He nodded toward another woman. "Come back later when she's gone. She pretends to shop, but she's a spy."

Whoever she was, she didn't work for us. Possibly she reported to Customs, but I doubt it. Either way, a moment later he threw her out of the store so that I, the spy, could shop. Not only did he fail to suspect me, he shared delicate information! My countenance and personality telegraphed a prodigious naïveté. It's a circumstance discouraging and frustrating, and I didn't mind at all using it against them.

Still, even with my airtight *Hee Haw* avatar, I couldn't get cocky. A couple of times during my stint with the firm, coworkers returned from a day on the streets and heard, when the elevator opened, "You've been burned." Our manager knew immediately because she had informants on the inside. That was a spotter's worst day of work and also his or her last. It's kind of like accidentally firing yourself.

Typically, though, the response was, "I figured." An agent knows when the jig is up. If you approach a shop and it closes its gates, you've been burned. If you turn around and a shopkeeper you've been watching is following to see where *you're* going, you've been burned. If passing one of the sentinel lookouts, who stand on stools at major intersections in Chinatown during the highly trafficked weekends, leads him to reach for his mobile phone and set off a chain reaction of cellular warnings that runs down Canal Street like those mountaintop bonfires in *The Return of the King*, you've been burned.

Game over.

In other words, I couldn't work every day. But it was summer, and in your twenties, that means weddings, which require plane tickets, gifts, and for me, that summer, two bridesmaids dresses. I was behooved by teal-green ruffles to seek supplementary employment. I picked up temp work here and there. And because I had experience waiting tables in college at a wing joint called Pantana Bob's—for which I wore a T-shirt that read "Bob's Got a Big Deck!"—I scored one shift a week at the legendary West Village brewpub Chumley's.

It was cush. The owner promised a set amount each shift, so if my tips were short, he'd pay out the difference from his pocket; decent guy. He rarely had to, though. The place stayed packed. Both locals and tourists competed to sit in a booth that might have been occupied by John Steinbeck, Jack Kerouac, Simone de Beauvoir, F. Scott Fitzgerald, J. D. Salinger, Willa Cather, e.e. cummings, William Burroughs, Norman Mailer, Ernest Hemingway, Edna St. Vincent Millay, or any other of the dozens of literary luminaries who are said to have haunted the windowless speakeasy either during or after its Prohibition heyday. It didn't matter that flies swarmed the back room, the jukebox featured only opera, or that sawdust inevitably found its way into your overpriced shepherd's pie and frequently flat beer. With a pedigree such as that, derelictions are deemed charming. I agreed. I loved the joint.

I discovered the venerable institution through Lou, the elder of my two older sisters, who lived in the West Village when I arrived in New York. She and her friends, many of whom went to college with her, took me under their collective wing as the kid sister they knew me to be—emphasis on *kid*. Lou and I are seven years apart, so those college pals hadn't seen me since the perm.

Actually, Lou and I hadn't seen much of each other either. She left for boarding school when I was eight. Of course, we visited over holidays and family vacations, but we didn't have a relationship outside of the family unit. It was different with my middle sister,

Tucker, but with Lou...I spent more of my cognitive childhood imagining her than experiencing her.

I remember trying to picture her New York apartment. In my mind, it had a tree-lined street and simple concrete stoop. I'd visualize ascending a dark and steep stairwell; I could see myself opening the door. I knew the layout of the fictional furniture and the color of the imaginary couch.

Of course, her real apartment was completely different, and hilariously smaller—particularly when, in addition to her and her roommate, I was there, which was all of the time. I'd come over to watch TV, or have a glass of wine, or just because I could. The first time we ordered takeout, I painstakingly separated out the duplicate menus in order to beef up my collection uptown, before Lou explained that New York restaurants don't deliver beyond their immediate area: "Did you think they'd get on the subway with your pad thai?"

She teased me a lot, but mostly she mothered me, which I guess I needed at the time because why else would I think it was OK to sleep over in her tiny double bed, like, once or twice a week? I would have hated me. She gave me a key, and occasionally I'd let myself in at three in the morning, when they were both asleep, have a snack, open Lou's door, and ask her to "scoot over."

But most of the times that I stayed were on nights when we'd been out together carousing in her neighborhood joints. Everywhere in the West Village was legendary. We went to Corner Bistro for the best burgers in the city, and to the White Horse Tavern, where Dylan Thomas drank himself to death. Lou and I stood in line for cupcakes at Magnolia Bakery and caught a scene of *Sex and the City* being shot on her block.

When my lease was up in August, I decided to move to the corner of Perry and Hudson streets. My friends thought I was crazy;

the apartment on Eighty-Seventh was a block from Central Park, had a private garden with a tree and a hammock, and my portion was $300 less a month than I'd be paying on Perry. Why was I moving to the West Village?

"I don't know," I said and shrugged my shoulders. "Sounds cool."

Unfortunately, Lou wasn't there anymore. She'd moved back to North Carolina the month prior. She lived in New York for seven years, but we overlapped for only one. Oh well, at least she'd had a chance to show me the ropes, for example, how to get *into* Chumley's.

The main entrance was hidden in the back of a courtyard on Barrow Street, and the back door was unmarked at 86 Bedford; during Prohibition, when a bribed cop called to warn the barkeep of an ensuing raid through the courtyard, the crowd was instructed to exit on Bedford, or to "eighty-six it," which is the origin of that famous idiom. Patrons could also escape through a secret bookcase that led to an alley. Apparently, F. Scott Fitzgerald and Zelda Sayre consummated their marriage in one of the booths. And it's where James Joyce wrote *Ulysses*.

Oh geez, oops: I'm lying again. Sorry: you're not diners. I guess, while working there, it became second nature. Those stories, and a dozen others phonier than a character in *The Catcher in the Rye*, were tossed to patrons thirsty for more than a pint. I heard some of them from other servers, a few from the walking-tour and bar-crawl guides who led their keeps inside, and most from curious patrons who'd picked up the apocryphal trivia elsewhere: travel books, blogs, drunkards at other neighborhood haunts. Everyone was in on it.

Here's the truth. There *is* an entrance at 86 Bedford, but the phrase "eighty-six it" had been in use—and in print—long before Chumley's opened. There was also a secret bookcase, but it went to the kitchen. And it's pretty well documented that James Joyce wrote *Ulysses* in Zurich and Paris. As for the young Fitzgeralds... I can't prove they didn't... and they *were* married in New York's St. Patrick's Cathedral... but still, sometimes you have to trust your gut, and mine thinks even Gatsby and Daisy wouldn't have boinked in a pub. As one of the walking-tour guides put it, "Writers are known to get drunk and embellish."

No one set out to spread distortions. It started innocently. In fact, I believed the tales myself until a fellow employee laughed at one of my questions and asked, "You *do* know that half of those stories are false?" But then, it became hard to stop—particularly when customers asked leading questions. One wanted to know if the ladies' room had once been a dumbwaiter that carried people to a gambling den on the second floor. Another had heard that, actually, the dumbwaiter went to the basement and was how they carried the booze inside. Or, according to someone else, that's what the trapdoor was for, since it connected to a tunnel that led to the rum-delivering boats. Still others pointed to that door in the floor and told their friends, "Runaway slaves used to climb through that hole because when this was a blacksmith's shop, it was a stop on the Underground Railroad."

And then they'd look up at me, all of them, with eager eyes, and ask, "Isn't that right?"

Um, er, thwlllpb, "Sure is! Neat, huh?" Tell them what they want to hear.

The only time I didn't play along, I instantly regretted it. While I distributed menus, a father told his children that this had been where Dylan Thomas died.

"Actually," I piped in, "you're thinking of the White Horse." His face sank, and so did his children's. What had I achieved? What mattered more: verifying a useless fact or giving them a memorable meal—one whose imagined worth exceeded the menu's prices?

Besides, I can't say for sure that Thomas *didn't* stop by Chumley's for one round before heading to the White Horse, just as it's impossible to prove that the blacksmith shop wasn't part of the Underground Railroad, or that the bookcase hadn't, at one point, led to the street. F. Scott Fitzgerald wrote, "Sometimes I don't know whether Zelda and I are real or whether we are characters in one of my novels."

And anyway, Dylan Thomas died in St. Vincent's Hospital.

So from that point forward, I just said yes to all of the legends. "I heard Fitzgerald wrote *Gatsby* here." He sure did, and in fact, you are sitting in the same booth. "Is it true that R.F.K. sketched out his presidential campaign platform in this bar?" Yeah, and would you believe it was in this exact booth!

You could have asked me anything. Did William Burroughs name *Naked Lunch* after Chumley's BLT? Is that the barstool where e.e. cummings gave up capital letters? Is this where a blind John Milton dictated *Paradise Lost* to his amanuensis?

You bet, and I don't want to blow your mind, but it was in this very booth.

Wait a second, the fictional you is thinking, Milton died before the West Village existed. Sure, but didn't you know that the dumbwaiter in Chumley's was once a time machine?

After escaping entrapment in the Pokémon-sheet cave, I cut down a block and moved swiftly on Walker Street toward the center of Chinatown, intuiting that my next assignment would be on the west end of Canal, where no one had seen me yet, and knowing that I'd need to reach it before the news of the last raid did. I called the office for the target and sure enough, it was still several blocks away. When I arrived, the goods on display were all anonymous, legal. I feared it was too late, but I milled about regardless.

A middle-aged woman standing nearby solicited advice about a wallet she considered.

"I can't believe it's real leather for this cheap," she giggled in a thick Long Island accent.

"It's not real," I told her, maintaining my harmless Southern drawl, but unable to disguise the skepticism.

"But it says so on the wallet," she said incredulously.

"That doesn't mean anything." I don't know why I chose this battle. I guess, sometimes I was bothered less by the counterfeiters—even though they annually steal around one billion tax dollars from New York City, support a system of illegal-immigrant indentured servitude, and occasionally fund terrorism—than I was by the willful naïveté of the bargain hunters. How could she believe that piece of junk was real? Were we looking at the same wallet? It had a plastic sheen. The stitching wasn't even in straight lines.

At this point, she shouted across the store to the vendor, intent on settling the dispute: "Is it real?"

"Of course," he said, "it says so on the label."

She looked up at me and actually said, "I told you so."

Whatever, I thought. *You are not my child.* Then I saw a man walk out of the back room with a thirty-gallon trash bag slung over his shoulder, and instantly stopped caring about the fool from Long Island.

It wasn't too late after all. They'd merely removed the contraband from the front room; only now were they excising it from the premises. I felt my heartbeat accelerate as I casually spun my back to him, a move that also allowed me to see which way he turned outside the door—I would have to follow. Then I flipped through the "real" wallets one more time, giving him a several-second head start, and pursued the tail.

Following people was the only time I didn't feel completely confident and comfortable on the job. When gathering intelligence, I could come and go as I pleased, depending on who was or wasn't looking. But while tailing a mark, I couldn't cut my own path. And I feared that would draw suspicion, betray me; no two people follow the exact same path.

I maintained a generous distance between us as we headed east, and I called the office to alert the raid team of a change in plans. On the other side of Broadway, he crossed south on Canal and then did what I'd feared he would seconds earlier: took a right on Cortland Alley. No one walks through Cortland Alley. It's a narrow passage that spans two blocks and has no storefronts. You might recognize it from appearing in movies whose scripts call for an alley that *no one walks through*. It is not the sort of grimy, dark, vermin-infested, less-traveled road down which a prim, tomato-pie-making, y'all-spewing gal from the sticks would, on a whim, mosey.

True to its nature, this morning Cortland Alley was empty. I lingered on the corner of Canal before turning, aiming to diminish the amount of time we'd be alone on the block, but I had to enter: The distance to the next intersection is long enough that if I waited until he arrived at it, and he turned, he'd have had an opportunity to turn again before I arrived, and I would've lost him for good. So I joined.

He never looked back. I reminded myself that criminals are dumb. After a few more blocks, he led me not to another handbag store, which was typically the case as ringleaders control several locations, nor to a warehouse-like storage facility, which is how we made the occasional major bust, but to a small innocuous food market on a side street. Everyone is in on it.

He nodded to a guy, who nodded back and then led him through a door behind the counter. I grabbed a produce baggie. The room was redolent of fish alive, dead, dried, and dying. Every piece of text contained within was written or printed in Chinese. I was the only Caucasian inside and desperately tried to appear as if I had a reason to be, as if I'd come for something specific. That ended up being three stocky white root vegetables, the least unfamiliar items for sale. Burdock? Parsnip? I have no idea what I fried and ate that night.

Confident that the contraband would not move again, I left the market and called in its address to my manager. When I met the team that night at the Irish pub, I heard they'd rolled into the grocery with a warrant an hour after I left. The bags were exactly where I'd said they'd be. Somebody bought me a beer.

The next day I worked at Chumley's, slinging burgers and returning beers when they became flies' watery graves. But the day after that I was back in Chinatown. I should've waited longer, let things cool. I cased a few stalls: usual shtick, usual scores. And then, near the intersection of Canal and Centre, a man in a baseball cap caught my eye and held it for a millisecond longer than I expected him to.

I felt it immediately. I continued in the same direction at a casual pace for a block and a half, and then looked over my shoulder. Sure enough, he was behind me—talking on his cell phone. To confirm what I already knew, I popped into another storefront or two, but, wouldn't you know: No one was selling knockoffs anymore that day, not even when I batted my eyelashes, drew out my "i"s, and talked about Jesus.

Returning to the office, I expected a burn notice, but when the elevator doors opened all I heard was, "Hey Jane." It's possible I was wrong but ... there's no way I was wrong. An agent knows. I must've blown my cover in the grocery; Baseball Cap must have been in that market.

On Canal Street, I drew no suspicion, because I looked like a tourist, sure, but also because the salesmen had an incentive to believe I was who I said I was: They wanted to sell bags. Just like the fool from Long Island believed the wallets were real because she *wanted* to have found a deal on a luxury item.

It was the incentive that had made me a good spy—not my own work—and no one in the grocery store had it. They saw my syrupy Southern-tourist persona for what it was: a knockoff unraveling at its haphazardly stitched seams.

I was too ashamed to tell my boss, so instead I removed my name from the remainder of the schedule and left.

Not long after that, upon entering my apartment building on the corner of Hudson and Perry, I walked upstairs and stuck my key in the lock, but it wouldn't turn. Duh, I thought, as I instantly realized my gaffe: wrong floor. I deduced the error quickly because I was familiar with the mistake; I made it about once a week that year. It was a strange and annoying affliction that has never struck me in any other of my many dwellings.

My place was on the third floor, first door at the top of the stairs. Sometimes I stuck my key in the right lock. Other times I tried to open the corresponding door on the second floor, and sometimes even the one on the fourth. My neighbors never said anything; I was mostly a nuisance to myself.

In this particular instance, however, after recently being burned, the pattern played out a little differently. When I yelled at myself in my head—*Geez, it's like you're a tourist in your own home!*—I saw that I was. The West Village wasn't home. I realized that I didn't even like it that much. In fact, I generally hung out in the bars and restaurants of other neighborhoods. I'd hardly decorated my room. The apartment felt counterfeit.

So I started thinking backward. If this seemed obvious now, but I hadn't noticed any of it before, then my ignorance must have been willful, which means I'd had an incentive—one whose imagined worth was so great, I'd gone more than $4,000 in debt paying rent in a neighborhood I couldn't afford.

OK, here is where I tell you that I lied one last time. The truth is this: I do know why I moved to the West Village. I was chasing Lou. Finally, *finally* I'd reached her, and suddenly she was gone again. But in the legendary West Village, I could retrace her steps. Whenever I fancied, I could pop into Magnolia for a chocolate cupcake or go dancing at Automatic Slims. I could eat burgers at Corner Bistro and tell myself with eager eyes, "I bet Lou sat here once... in this very booth!"

I had spent so many years imagining her before, it was easy to slip back into the habit. But I wasn't chasing her; I was chasing her narrative, trying to consume her authentic experience—an inherently inauthentic pursuit. No two people follow the exact same path. And I couldn't even be certain the narrative was true. I'd cobbled the account together from anecdotes apocryphal and embellished by drink. I had the right key but it was in the wrong lock. If the world is made of narratives, then it was time I write my own.

And I may as well start from the beginning.

Dive

I Think You
Dropped This

"**D**ammit! Get back here, Dammit!" My grandfather used to shout those words from his front porch every night. He was calling the dog inside. The dog's name was Dammit. My mother and Aunt Jane had begged for a puppy, but my grandfather said no, until he finally relented, on the condition that he be allowed to name it, which he did with the express purpose of wailing curse words into the neighborhood.

One night, Dammit—or, Dit, as he was known to everyone else—didn't come home. It was an inevitability the family had anticipated since the first time their next-door neighbors fed the dog filet mignon. He liked to visit the Hermans, and one time when he did, Elise Herman had her butler prepare steak. After that, Dit began every morning by trotting next door for breakfast. Once he correctly assumed that there might also be filet for dinner, Dit ate all of his meals with the Hermans. He liked it there. So when Elise placed a blue-satin, down-stuffed pillow next to her own bed, Dit moved in for good.

Decades later, when I graduated from college and decided to leave North Carolina for New York, Aunt Jane exclaimed, "Don't go! You'll have a ball and stay. I have a friend who moved there forty years ago and never got married, and no one ever saw her again. You know that happens to a lot of girls."

"Wait a second," I interjected, knowing I had her trapped. "What's the fear, that you'll miss me or that I'll be an old maid?"

She thought for a few seconds and responded, "No, I know you'll get married because you're not fat." Then she announced that she was late for a bridge game and hung up the phone.

As reluctant as I am to further expound upon an analogy that likens me to a dog, I must admit that when I first came to New York, I wandered around all wide-eyed and trusting, assuming that everyone wanted to scratch my belly. It makes sense: I'd come from the Land of Belly Scratchers, the South, where 50 percent of the vocabulary is comprised of heartwarming adages. We are a population who whistles, says good morning to inanimate objects, and ascertains the presence of angels. There is always someone who's the last to stop clapping; that person is usually Southern.

This doesn't necessarily make us nicer people. Obviously, human beings are more complicated than that. I'm just saying that this is the way we behave: People think we're drunk when we're sober. I was reared to act like a golden retriever. Which is why, in at least one instance during my first week in New York, I literally fetched.

While walking up Eighth Avenue, I noticed a piece of paper fall from the pocket of a man walking a few yards ahead of me. Prescription? Important receipt? I ran to pick it up and catch him.

"Excuse me, sir?" I touched the back of his shoulder and said with pep, "I think you dropped this." But before he even turned around—while "dropped this" repeated in distorted deep-voiced slow motion in my ears—I realized my mistake. He'd littered. And I had been horrifically naive. I steeled myself for the ensuing humiliation, but when he turned around, his face held only contempt.

Double eureka: he thought I was being sarcastic. Because we were in New York, not a Disney film, he'd never considered sincere to be an option. And therefore, he assumed I was handing him trash to make a self-righteous point. I thought I was wagging my tail; he saw a stray with rabies.

Scrunching his brow, he said only one word: "Really?"

But I couldn't think of a response that might not also be misconstrued as sarcasm. So instead, I dropped the litter back on the ground. There you go, Borden! Why stop at offending one man, when you can disrespect an entire city?

Walking away red in the face and chastising my own gullibility, I thought, *Lesson learned.* But of course, that wasn't true; I'd only come to understand one symptom of a much larger and deep-seated problem, which would, like all buried issues, manifest eventually. Mine arrived a few days later in the form of jaw pain.

"Ow," I said, rubbing my cheeks and climbing into bed.

"What hurts?" my roommate asked.

"My face."

"What happened?" she asked.

"I don't know."

"Do you think it's stress?"

"But I haven't even started work yet," I said. "I spent all day in a bakery."

"Maybe it's from crunching," she offered. "Have you been eating a lot of raw vegetables?"

"I spent all day in a bakery."

A couple of days later, it blossomed into headaches.

"Maybe you're grinding your teeth at night," a friend suggested.

No, because it was better in the morning and worse at night.

"Have you been wearing headbands?" my mother asked.

No.

"Maybe you took a strange exercise class?" she offered.

No, because, OK, I was spending every day at bakeries.

Then, while walking down Amsterdam Avenue, a passerby made eye contact with me and recoiled in that way that silently says "You are embarrassing yourself." You know the look. The eyes bulge, the lower lip curls down, and the entire head pulls slightly back and to the left, as if there's a God of Awkward Social Encounters who's tugging the person's ear in warning.

Why would she do that? All I did was smile at her.

Oh my God of Awkward Social Encounters! I *smiled* at her! And it wasn't a halfhearted, obligatory lip twitch that says, "Oops, we accidentally locked eyes." Mine was earnest. Without realizing it, I'd been staring for half a block, patiently waiting for her to return my gaze so I could shoot her one heat-seeking grin. And then it sunk in. No wonder my jaw was sore: I'd been smiling at *everyone*. In New York, that's more than a dozen per block, times a ten-block walk, is at least 120 per outing. I had a new exercise regimen after all.

In my hometown, Greensboro, North Carolina, everyone smiles at one another. Without exception. In the aisles of the Harris Tee-ter grocery store, in lines at the movie thee-ate-er, even in cars— stoplights are long. I realize, in retrospect, how strange it is, and how time-consuming. If you know the person, you pause to speak. If not, you say "Hello" or ask "How you?" At the least, you wave. Not the standard arm-raised, palm-forward, side-to-side swish. The preferred method is to place your arm out parallel to the ground, palm facing down, and then vigorously wag the hand up and down from the wrist as if you're suppressing a putrid smell or doing that thing homophobes do when pretending to be gay. You're probably thinking only women wave like this. Men do too. Even the homophobes.

We're real-life versions of those animatronic Teddy Ruxpin bears: Regardless of our intentions, out of context, the behavior is creepy. It may be nice to make contact with one stranger on a sunny knoll, but to do so with a dozen on a grimy city block is terrifying. I must have looked like a maniac, bobbing my head this way and that, forcing onto everyone my hysterical grin. If I were a man, I would have been maced.

You can't walk around New York going, "Hi, I'm Jane Borden. Will you be my friend?" Fifth Avenue is not a high-five tunnel. I felt like a total asshead. And I could hear Aunt Jane standing on her porch screaming, "Asshead! Get back here, Asshead!"

But it was just a habit, right? Obviously I didn't want to be pals with eight million people. I mean, I kind of do, but no, that's absurd: When would we all get coffee? It's simply not possible. So I would have to change, assimilate, or be shunned by the herd. It wouldn't be easy.

I remember standing in a line somewhere a few weeks later—it was probably a bakery—behind a man wearing a worn-out black T-shirt from R.E.M.'s Green tour. *Oh, man,* I thought, *I have a shirt from that tour too! I should tell him.*

Relax, Borden. He probably found that tee at a thrift store. He doesn't want to talk to you. Leave him alone.

"Stand in the place where you live..." I started singing in my head and thinking about the video. Maybe he remembers the choreography!

Get a grip: He doesn't want to dance with you. He doesn't want to bond. This was harder than I'd anticipated. I tried to think about something else, likely a muffin. My efforts at cognitive redirection backfired, however, by opening the door to my subconscious, which quickly revisited the Green situation. When I emerged from my reverie, my hand was in the air, an inch and a half second away from tapping him on the shoulder.

My God, the line was moving slowly. I started feeling fidgety, tweaking out. Teddy Ruxpin was bottling, sweating, about to explode.

But soon the man reached the front of the line. And then he left.

I'd done it: successfully silenced my urge to lick the face of everything that breathes. Although my heart hurt a little, I felt a sense of pride. There was no other choice: Old Yeller had to be shot.

But then I thought about the countless others at whom I'd unconsciously grinned during that first week. The ones who hadn't recoiled. Most of them must have at least politely acknowledged me or I would have cottoned to my behavior sooner. Maybe some of them were even secretly glad to smile back.

So I struck a deal with my new home. I have hardened. I turn a lot of opportunities into ghosts. You have to; there is no other way. But sometimes, when the circumstances are right, say, a quiet block on a Sunday night or an empty subway stairwell, I'll pick one approaching, unsuspecting pedestrian, wait until we're within a few feet of each other, and then stick my hand out—not a limp-wristed, high-pitched, produce-aisle wag, but a commanding, decisive, palm-facing-forward call for a high five. And I'll tell you this, contrary to whatever stereotypes you think you know about New Yorkers, I've never been denied contact.

Dancing with
the Enemy

*T*he most perfect relationship I've ever had was with a total stranger. I love strangers. When I don't know you, I don't know your faults. And you don't know mine. For the brief time we interact, we're flawless.

The notion is similar to the way some grade-school teachers tabulate behavior scores by starting each student at a hundred and knocking off points for transgressions throughout the year. For instance, if my third-grade teacher had employed such a system, I might have lost ten points for talking during his tests, five for fomenting resistance to our monthly fluoride rinses, and twenty when I accidentally called him a whore.

"Do you know what that means?" he asked.

"A wild pig," I responded.

He shook his head and handed me the dictionary.

My point is that, before the plummeting kinetic energy of our faults takes hold, our new relationship is full of potential. I don't know that you're the kind of person who pockets crackers from restaurants. Neither do you know that I sleep with a noise machine and also earplugs to drown out the noise machine.

As strangers, we are perfect. And will remain that way. Until I inevitably call you a whore.

So: this relationship. It happened in a bar on the Upper East Side one night toward the end of my first year in the city. In a place as diverse as New York, the bar scene uptown is surprisingly homogeneous, full of twenty-two-year-olds who come to the city for a postgrad degree in drinking and one-night stands.

Our parents encourage the journey, saying "Go and have fun!"— the silent supporting clause of that statement being "Before you settle down back here." So coveys of college grads recycle themselves in overpriced adapted two-bedrooms on York Avenue. We treat our time in New York like a rite of passage, a year spent in the woods. The problem is that most of us hang out exclusively with other Southerners in frat bars on the Upper East Side. We don't want to be in New York specifically; we just want to be somewhere else for a while.

This is "the plan." It's not the sort you set in advance, but rather, realize after the fact you'd unwittingly followed. No one says, "I'll move to New York and procrastinate life." Nevertheless, that's precisely what we do. We say, and believe, that we came to the city to seek opportunity, take a chance. But mostly we're just killing time until last call. Or, at least, that's what I was doing.

But I didn't know it until that night in the bar on the Upper East Side, when the DJ's playlist—"Y.M.C.A.," "I Will Survive," "Like a Virgin"—sounded like a mix from a Phi Delt late night. That is when this opaque plan revealed itself to me. Like many a revelation, it came after I'd gone into a bathroom to accidentally smoke half of a joint.

Upon exiting, and complaining to the next girl in line about the stoner who must have preceded me, I heard it: the song lyric that can make the ears of any American girl prick up.

"I got chiiiiiills, they're multiplying."

Most young people in our country can't find Kuwait on a map, but we all know the words and battle-of-the-sexes choreography to the penultimate song in *Grease*. I stood motionless, stunned by the marijuana, in an estrogen stampede. Responding to the song's war cry, a brigade of calf-high black boots carried girls to the dance floor just in time to gather on one side, point an accusing finger at their testosterone-filled counterparts and croon with all the gravitas they could muster from a semester in poli sci, *"You better shape up!"*

I circumnavigated the dance floor, enjoying the show and filling out the actors' résumés. A girl in a pink cardigan was flipping her long hair from side to side on cue with the "ooh, ooh, ooh"s. She looked like an Allison.

Allison lived on Eighty-Second Street and York, I supposed. Although she'd wanted a job in fashion, she'd wound up in PR. The girl with whom she shimmied was definitely a boy name: a Blake or an Eason. Maybe Hadley, Tinsley, or Dabney. Southerners do this a lot. It sounds like a boy's name but really it's a last name, typically the mother's maiden, and actually it's the girl's middle name.

It was harder to guess the guys' names, as I assumed that several of them went by the nickname Chip or Trip. Of their jobs, I could be more certain: finance, finance, finance, money management, and finance. The three leaning against the column had been together all night, predominantly in that spot. This led me to believe they were fresh off the boat and probably living in what I've come to call a Halfway Frat: an apartment that, like a halfway house, provides living quarters to recently deinstitutionalized persons, in this case college graduates who've moved to New York.

There are two categories of HalfFrats. The first is a "Willing." Year after year, a lease is passed down, or willed, from last year's alums to this year's graduating seniors—who must still pay real-estate agents their finder's fees. Such was the case with my first place in the city. I moved into, with two college roommates, an Upper West Side apartment, which had previously been occupied by three girls who'd just graduated from Carolina, which had previously been occupied by three girls who'd just graduated from Carolina. Farther west along the block was a literal halfway home, one of many in a program designed to sprinkle low-income housing throughout the city in brownstones and town houses. If its residents saved their wine corks for future craft projects, then we had a lot in common indeed.

The second breed of HalfFrat I call a "Revolving Door." This is generally a one-in-one-out system. Whenever one roommate moves, a graduating friend replaces him, which means that the lease need not change hands. However, in accordance with the friend-in-need maxim, and also the drunk-dude-sleeps-anywhere theorem, Revolving Doors typically feature more tenants than bedrooms. When my friend Sammy moved up from Chapel Hill, he took up residence with several of his older Phi Delt brothers in a closet in their East Village Revolving Door. Although it was a three-bedroom, at any time, four to five people were passing out there.

And every weekend they had a party, frequently with a keg and almost always with KC and the Sunshine Band playing while the television was on but muted. I know because I was usually there. I "knew" those people in the Upper East Side bar because I am them. For example, my sister has a boy name: Tucker. It's my mother's maiden name, and actually, Tucker is her middle, but my parents chose to call her by it because her first name is Russell. So really she has two boy names. And technically, the third Borden sister, although it is short for Louisa, goes by Lou, which is a man's name too—or, at least, all others going by it, excluding my grandmother, have either been male or a fixture in a bathroom. I'm surprised my parents didn't name me Tom. Or Sink.

What I didn't yet know about my college crowd—there were a couple dozen of us in the city at the time—is that after a year, most of them would be gone. They'd start saying they were tired: tired of hangovers, piles of garbage, and the stench of urine; tired of screaming neighbors and the constant rumbling of trucks in their dreams. Tired of New York. So they'd leave. Budweiser is cheaper in Raleigh.

Then the halfway-home bar would fill with their replacements.

But on the night in question, I didn't know this yet. Or, I guess I was starting to figure it out. Let's put it this way: I'd been getting chills, and they were multiplying.

I moved around among the dancers unnoticed, or so I thought. While counting the number of chinos twisting in rhythm, I noticed a pair that was still. I raised my gaze and locked eyes with a young man standing on the other side of the dance floor, my perfect stranger.

I must have inadvertently swayed my head, as I'm wont to do, because he began to mimic it. I put my hands on my hips. He put his hands on his hips. Testing the commitment level, I squatted into an elaborate plié.

Oh, he was game.

Before I had the chance to safely distance myself from the situation by mocking it, he thrust one pointed index finger into the air and we disco-walked to the center of the floor. The ensuing minutes of dance were fantastically elaborate and completely in sync. Without speaking or planning, we knew the routine.

He spun me with his right arm and at the end of my revolution, I dropped my left hand to my side, catching his, which was waiting to lead me through a side-by-side shimmy.

While I pretended to check an invisible watch, and blow imaginary bangs from my eyes, he circled me, flicking fingers like guns on either side of his waist.

When I inflicted only the slightest bit of pressure on his shoulder, he intuited that he was to kneel so I could split-leg leapfrog over him.

By this point we'd attracted attention. The crowd was also in sync; it parted just in time to witness the most successful *Dirty Dancing* jump I've ever tried. I'm not saying he carried me, but I did catch air. And then, suddenly, it became clear that this particular sock hop would culminate in lip lock, as if that had been the point all along. So as the final chords reverberated through the bar's cheap sound system, he spun me one more time and led me into the portended dip. Then he leaned in and kissed me. It didn't occur to me to resist. It wasn't awkward and it wasn't a joke, but it wasn't sexual, either. We were professional Sandys and Dannys, and this was just part of the act.

But I hadn't thought beyond that point. What would happen when he pulled me up? I knew that my John Travolta and I wouldn't get into a car that inexplicably takes flight. But I feared we might embark on a journey with an even higher crash incidence: conversation. I was terrified of sullying our otherwise perfect exchange. What if he wanted to know my name, or worse, my number? What if he were gay—what straight guy knows *Dirty Dancing* choreography?

This was a fight-or-flight moment...except I was trapped prone in his arms two feet from the floor, so both fight and flight would have ended in concussion. I closed my eyes, a ridiculous tactic, I know. But I didn't want to see with whom I'd swapped spit. I wanted him to remain forever frozen in suspended animation, like a woman in a dip or a chapter in a book on a shelf.

Then he did the unexpected. He pulled me up, released my hand, stepped backward, and silently bowed. I bent my left knee, pointed my right foot out in front of me, and, with all of the gravitas garnered from debutante-ball training, curtsied. Then we both turned and walked in opposite directions.

Apparently I didn't know those people at all. Which made me wonder, What else do I not know? So I grabbed my coat, hailed a cab, and never went back.

The Cartoon

Assassin

"Jane, I want to tell you something. This is important. Don't wear your pearl earrings on the subway. A criminal will rip them from your ears. My friend Nancy Lily was in a taxi in New York and it was summertime, I guess, because the window was down, and somebody reached in and yanked her gold necklace off her neck! She could have been choked! She wasn't; it broke. But they ran off with it. So don't wear jewelry on the bus. Or on the subway. Just don't wear it at all."

"Yes ma'am."

"Now, costume jewelry is fine. Unless it *looks* real, and then I wouldn't wear that, either."

"Yes ma'am."

"And don't ride the subway after dark. Promise me you'll take taxis. Anytime after nine p.m. Don't walk anywhere!"

"Yes ma'am."

"Good. *And don't look at anybody!!*"

That's my aunt Jane again, giving me advice before I moved to New York, which was a while ago, so you're probably assuming that the above is a reimagining. It is not. Neither, however, did I record and transcribe our chat. How do I remember the script? I heard it anew a couple of days later, again a week after that, a dozen more times through the following months, and about once or twice a year since. Like a frat guy with a classic comedy film, I have favorite bits I like to quote.

First, I love how, in spite of the number of times I've previously heard the drama unfold, she always clarifies that her friend with the necklace did not choke. Spoiler alert: she was fine. I'm also particularly fond of my aunt's suggestion that I should continue to wear costume jewelry, as if to say, "The criminals can't keep us from accessorizing." The best part, though, is her outro, "Don't look at anybody." Sometimes it varies. "Look down" and "Keep your eyes on the ground" are also in the mix, but, regardless, the intimation is the same: New Yorkers are wild animals; they will attack if provoked.

In short, she worries, thinks the city is very dangerous. And I think she is hilarious—she once paused midscript, pulled the phone away from her mouth, and shouted to my uncle, "Lucius! You have to remember to hide the barbecue potato chips from me!" So I ignored her advice. I shouldn't have. As it turned out, my life was in danger the instant my feet touched Manhattan pavement. That's when I was hit by a car.

The taxi I hailed at LaGuardia Airport delivered me to the northeast corner of Union Square, an intersection that I have since come to believe was designed by M. C. Escher, and I, with a duffel bag on my back as big and awkward as the grin on my face, opened the door onto traffic. "Other side!" shouted my driver.

Here is where things get fuzzy. I don't know why I ignored his admonition—perhaps I mistook it for an overenthusiastic version of "Catch you on the flip side"; or maybe I thought he was screaming at the tape deck—but ignore it I did, and then stepped directly in front of a moving vehicle. Thanks to agile footwork, mine on the pavement and the oncoming driver's on the brakes, I got off with a graze. It was more of a bump-and-jump. The offending automobile didn't even stop. I landed on the intersection's island, blinked once or twice, and looked back at the car just in time to catch the gaze of its stunned passenger, like an apparition through the glass.

"Other side"? Yeah, of the realm of the living. I may have been deaf to every warning preceding the incident, but I heard its follow-up message loud and clear: "I'll get you next time."

Uh-oh. This was worse than my aunt had imagined. Criminals were merely one component of a much bigger foe: the city itself. That's when I realized New York was out to get me. The city isn't evil; it's simply in its nature to destroy. It can't help itself. Kind of like the god of the Old Testament. Except New York is craftier, enjoys the chase. It will sneak up behind you, giggling, and stuff dynamite in your backpack. And if you happen to spin around too soon, it will hide its weapon, look the other way, and whistle. It's a coy killer, a lethal coquette—when caught in the act, New York bites its lip and twirls its hair, and all you can say is, "Oh, New York, you're *so* bad!"

"New York is sorry," it will say, in its adorable E.T.-like way of speaking in the third person.

"It's all right," you reply, because you can't stay mad. "Just promise not to do it again."

"New York promises," it says, but you know its fingers are crossed.

And sure enough, you later find a skull-and-crossbones bucket propped above your door. The city relishes its perdition. It's a gremlin, a cartoon assassin.

It's the villain in a 1980s video game: In order to keep us from stealing its coins, it throws poisonous mushrooms and deadly beetles in our paths. Most residents learn quickly to jump out of the way. But not I. During my first couple of years in Manhattan, I was foiled by them all.

Once, while carrying two laptops and headed to a sales call for my first job at an Internet start-up, I lodged the kitten heel of my right boot in a sidewalk grate obscured by the snow, and slapped the ground like an inverted rake. Another time, craning to see an art installation driving down the street on a flatbed truck, I walked into a pole. In fact, I frequently rammed into poles—and fire hydrants, bike racks, trash cans, orange traffic cones. Anything beneath eye level made contact with my groin. I was a live-action *America's Funniest Home Video.*

A gust of wind covered my fresh vanilla ice cream cone with dirt and trash. A falling Diet Coke can—origin unknown—bounced off my head. It was empty, but still: That is absurd. I'm not making this up. I was under constant cartoonish attack. But why? Why me? Everyone else seemed to get through their days unfazed. While I moved frenetically, lost my footing, tripped, wobbled, and splat, the other pedestrians remained stone-faced through the assault, hardly adjusting their gaits or paths. And I'd wonder, What the hell do they know?

It couldn't be that they'd memorized the board, because the

board is constantly changing. One day a pothole is on the left side of the intersection and the next day it's on the right. Scaffolding goes up and down. There's a fountain in front of *every* financial institution in midtown, and a Starbucks on each block. The only reliable landmark was the World Trade Center. Even so, knowing which way was south, while crossing an intersection, didn't keep me from stepping into the wire netting of a slaughtered, abandoned umbrella. It captured my foot like a bear trap. I dragged it all the way across Houston, limping and shaking my leg, before I could beat off the zombie arachnid.

In fact, in that incident, seeking a landmark had been the source of my downfall; for an instant, I stopped paying attention to my immediate surroundings. That's what makes the city such a clever goblin beastie: Not only does it put you in an environment where, with one distraction, you're toast; it then fills that environment with screaming, blinking distractions, daring you to lose your concentration. One night, I took a left on Broadway and fell into a sinkhole of paparazzi flashbulbs following Uma Thurman, who'd come to see the magician David Blaine, who'd trapped himself inside a hunk of ice—in the middle of Times Square.

If that scene ever occured in a small Southern hamlet, the town would rename itself Uma-Blaineville, Home of the Ten-Story Neon Pepsi Ad, and tourists would spend entire days strolling through the wax-figure exhibit built to commemorate the event. But in New York I had only a split second to glance at the circus lest I be trampled by the crowd, run over by a car, or electrocuted by a beverage on its way to fight Godzilla.

It's too dangerous to dwell on any moment in New York because something else of consequence is always on its heels. "Oh my gosh," I'd say to myself while walking to work at that start-up, Foodline .com, "check out that corporate dude riding his bike in a suit and Ugg boots—ha!...Except no, laugh later, because watch out for these guys carrying a sheet of glass across your path. Cool: The Flatiron Building is reflected in it from...Stop! File that image away, and instead avoid these high school kids making out in the middle of the street. Wow, her tongue is all the way out of her...Wait, not now. Right now look out for that—"

Whap!

Seriously, my hips and thighs were a menagerie of infrastructure-induced bruises; the city was beating the crap out of me. I know that life isn't fair, but it was a lot fairer before the Great Groin Assault of 2001. And if I couldn't get in sync with the flow of the streets, poisonous mushrooms and all, then maybe I didn't belong. Maybe I should just go home. I didn't want to. But clearly New York was trying to weed me out; I'm surprised I was never rammed in the pelvis with a gardening spade.

As it turns out, though, there is a silver lining around pole thwacking. It is by nature a behavior-altering stimulus. Eventually, when I hit one, it hit me: My problem was that I had misunderstood the phrase "watch where you're going." I was failing on the streets of New York because I'd been looking for impediments in my environment, when I should have clocked the faces of people successfully avoiding those obstacles. I had neglected to tap into the hive brain.

Here's how it works. Instead of scanning 360 degrees for danger, the potential of which is too voluminous and varied to manage alone, one covers only his or her immediate path—including fellow pedestrians therein. This way, the responsibility of assessing the landscape, knowing what to ignore and from what to run, is shared among the hive, allowing each bee to go about its duties. For example, if people ahead of you avoid a swath of concrete, you can deduce, even if you cannot see, the presence of something that might attack your crotch.

So, actually, *all* we do is look at each other. Aunt Jane was wrong. It's precisely how we stay alive. If a zoo-escaped gorilla is behind me, I will receive that information in the facial expression—terror or lack of terror—of the person walking toward me. A dozen times a second, this silent conversation transpires:

"Gorilla behind me?"

"Nope. You're safe. Me?"

"Nah."

Gorilla? Gorilla? Gorilla? Gorilla?

It's so efficient; it doesn't even require eye contact. What beautiful cooperation is born from the perpetually imminent threat of death. It's our form of the trust fall. I run to catch a subway train only if someone a hundred yards ahead of me in the tunnel does. Who needs traffic lights? Just cross when other people cross—or rather, when other *bees* cross; the behavior of tourists and rookies must always be ignored.

This city may praise individuality, but its residents are a herd. When one walks up Seventh Avenue, she is stepping behind one person, in front of another, around a couple holding hands, underneath a window washer, over the heroin addict nodding off, and between two piles of poo. New York offers only a prepositional life. No action exists without a modifier.

Buildings don't even have solitary identities. No one cares about the specific address of a restaurant on Sixth Avenue; they only need to know that it's between Seventeenth and Eighteenth streets. Entire neighborhoods are designated by what's around them rather than what's in them: SoHo is the area "south of Houston," TriBeCa is the "triangle below Canal," and SoBro is a Realtor's transparent attempt to draw yuppies to the South Bronx. Just as every plank on a train track is nailed to another, so will every person in Times Square get shoved about.

I became obsessed with the New York hive brain, which was somewhat surprising as I was currently enjoying my escape from its North Carolina counterpart, a group mind whose effect is summed up thusly: Everyone knows everything about everyone. Scientists couldn't prove whether or not it "takes a village" to rear a child where I'm from, because it would be impossible to devise a control group.

And I use the word "rear" instead of "raise," because, as my grammarian mother reminds me, "chickens are raised; children are reared." Wherever I went, people knew me. The amount of eyes in the backs of heads of the number of mothers and fathers standing sentinel over the locales of my youth would have rendered Big Brother redundant.

They watched each other, too. That's just how it is in a small town. There is no unfamiliar vista. However Orwellian the effect, the intentions are predominantly innocent. Sure, some are gossips, and yes, schadenfreude does live, in spite of sounding foreign, in many Southern homes, but for the most part, those stereotypes are false. Southerners are no more nosy or meddlesome than suburbanites in other geographical locations. The reason our group mind is more consuming than most of its counterparts is simply because these familiar vistas exist in space *and* time. These families have been up in each other's beeswax since the *Mayflower* landed. If Jung had studied the heroes in our dreams, he'd have discovered they all wear bow ties.

Around one corner from my parents' house on Carlisle Road in Greensboro was my mother's aunt Janie (my aunt Jane was named for *her*), and around the other corner was the family of my mother's aunt Emily, which was next door to the house where Janie and Emily had grown up with my grandmother, who lived six blocks away.

My dad grew up in Goldsboro, North Carolina, in the house

where his father was born, which his grandfather had built, a few houses down from the home where he'd been reared. Of the six houses on the block, all were owned by kin.

This was the world I was accustomed to. Then, suddenly, I was among eight million strangers, and the only one who knew my mother's maiden name was a bank teller. *I loved it.* I wore ratty T-shirts and cursed. I sat with my legs sprawled wide open and engaged in all manner of activities beyond the pale of my grooming.

I had jammed my own GPS radar and was living languorously off the grid. Yes, the bad behavior was refreshing, but it was not the source of my joy. What I really relished was the feeling that no one was "studyin' me."

On George Street, my grandparents had a housekeeper and cook named Alease. She worked seven days a week until my grandmother switched Sunday to a half day, a move that angered the neighbors because it tacitly required that they do the same for their servants. It was a different time.

Although Alease died before I was born, I've adopted many of her stories and sayings. Whenever my uncle and his friends caused mischief, by spraying the gardening hose while she was trying to kill a chicken, untying her apron strings while she plucked the carcass, or exhibiting any behavior designed explicitly to annoy someone doing a job that grocery stores hadn't yet made obsolete, she'd respond, "I ain't studyin' you." That is, keep it up if you like, but don't expect to get a rise out of me; I don't care.

No one in New York studied me. I could stand on a subway platform in full-body Day-Glo paint with a cat on my head reciting the elements on the periodic table—I'm the one who's reciting, not the cat...no, hell, sure, the cat's reciting the periodic table—and still the commuters would continue reading their *Post*s. And on the chance that someone did look up and disapprove, or judge, or call Ripley's Believe It or Not, I wouldn't care anyway because he or she would never see me again. I understand that I am not the first person to meditate on this quality of anonymity in New York, but that doesn't diminish the electric thrill of experiencing it firsthand.

Janie—my late great-aunt; for the record, there are currently five Janes living—used to call picking your teeth, applying lipstick, or scratching your head "homework," things you don't do in front of other people. After a few months in New York, I had witnessed each of those happen on a subway, in addition to fingernail clipping and over-the-clothes heavy petting, which can only mean one thing: Wherever New Yorkers are, they feel at home. What tourists regard as exhibitionism, locals herald as the inalienable right to treat the city like a bedroom. Therefore, those who stare at others on the streets of New York are the urban equivalent of Peeping Toms.

Succeeding in the hive means knowing the difference between studyin' and checking in. Now that I knew—and had learned to use the latter to avoid becoming intimate with every municipal erection—I'd really be able to enjoy my new success. Or so I thought. It's true that, once I joined the hive, the street-level threats diminished. But the hijinks on the whole continued. I had not defeated the Cartoon Assassin. Duh: I'd only made it to level two, where the game was harder and the hazards more menacing.

For example, I found myself locked out of my apartment at four in the morning, when I swore I'd put the keys in my purse. I slipped on a spot of lotion and fell gangly down the spiral staircase of that apartment, though both of my roommates denied having moisturized that day. And isn't it a little coincidental that the same week I moved into my second apartment, the carbon monoxide detector broke?

It went beyond the home. When the Internet bubble burst,

Foodline folded; they still owe me thousands. Next, one of my former clients hired me to manage her restaurant; it closed shortly thereafter. So I picked up extra work cleaning a theater in Chelsea, until the day when, while sitting on a toilet in the pitch black because the lightbulb was shot, a full-sized mirror fell from the door and shattered on my head, leaving a shard a centimeter from the major vein in my right wrist.

A mirror shattered on my head! That's the horror version of a Lewis Carroll tale. What the hell? Why was New York out to get me? I didn't know how much more I could take. It felt as if I were the enemy, as if New York were fulfilling a personal vendetta. And I have to admit: The city had good reason to seek revenge.

This is when I confirm an ugly rumor, when I put away my pride and admit something disgusting: Southerners still harbor a childish contempt for the North. It's insolent and arrogant, but nonetheless true. While growing up, we threw around the word "Yankee" with disdainful relish. And when we did, no one ever confused the discussion for one about baseball—even though baseball is also brash, gauche, and unaware of which direction the dessert spoon faces.

Oh dear, it's so embarrassing! You'd think that, after more than a hundred and fifty years, we'd have buried the hatchet, but notions of Northern aggression persist. The fear is not of a literal invasion. No one wants to secede or form a militia, except maybe in Texas, but as all Southerners know, Texas doesn't count. What's happening now is a culture war. High-society Southerners think New Yawkers have no class, no taste, no appreciation for lacy duvet covers and pastel smocking. They fear an invasion of Yankee conventions and habits, so they protect their own the best they can: by closely monitoring imports and exports.

My two older sisters went to boarding school in Connecticut and, as a result, returned for summers and holidays with subtle changes in their accents. Barbarians at the gate! Some or all of every sentence they uttered would be parroted back with gross exaggeration. Their friends looked for it, waiting to pounce. The way they said "you guys" instead of "y'all" wasn't just different; it was wrong.

I was as bad. Among my crowd at the University of North Carolina was only a handful of Northerners. Most of them assimilated instantly, due to incessant needling, but not Brett. And so we'd let him have it: for the club music in his car, the product in his hair, and the fact that, in the late 1990s, he had a cell phone. A cell phone: what a self-defeating reason to mock someone! "Ooh, look at you with your fancy piece of efficient technology. What are you, ahead of the curve? What are you gonna do, effortlessly stay connected with people? Brett and convenience sitting in a tree ... k-i-s-s-i-n-g."

As someone who fights the image of the simple Southerner, I probably shouldn't have told you that. But honesty heals all wounds, right? As such, New York should own up to its own stereotyping, which in at least one case has been institutionalized. While wandering through the dioramas at the American Museum of Natural History on Central Park West, I noticed that, of all the natural habitats re-created in the North American section, only one depicted a human among the flora and fauna. It was the southeastern coastal display, a picture of a swampy section of the Coosawhatchie River, beside which catbrier grows and wild turkeys wander, and along which floats a rude wooden boat carrying a man wearing, no joke, a straw hat and overalls. The literature beneath identifies thirty-seven species in the exhibit, including *Magnolia grandiflora*, *Pinus palustris*, and *Terrapene carolina*, but nowhere mentions *Barefoot hillbillyus*—as if we wouldn't notice. I bet the *Deliverance* theme plays on the audio tour.

Go ahead and add that to the many ways in which New York seemed to be asking me, during my first years in its den, "Who's laughing now, redneck?"

Fine, fine, fair enough. I surrendered to New York: "I'll take my lashings and like it, just leave me alone!" What else could I have done, fought back? There is no fighting New York; no slingshot could fell that giant. It's an activity as futile as screaming at the ocean. In an episode in the second season of TV's *The Osbournes*, Ozzy tries to dig a fire pit on the beach outside his California home. But as he nears completion, the tide encroaches and spoils his effort. That is when, in what must be the most poetic moment in the history of reality television, Osbourne—a quaint combination of infantile and feral—challenges the ocean itself. "Fuck!" he screams and then plants his bare feet in the foam, faces the void, and commands it, "Go to Alaska!" He beats the surf with his fists, shouting, "No, no, no, no. You fucking asshole ocean! No!" I dare Ozzy Osbourne to walk through Times Square during rush hour in the rain.

Besides, New York would figure out sooner or later that I wasn't the enemy. If I were sincerely bigoted toward the North, I wouldn't have moved there; I wouldn't have become an export myself. Of course I don't hate Yankees! How can you hate someone you don't even know? And anyway, the longer I stayed, the more I fell in love with the idiosyncrasies I'd previously mocked. The loudness. The lewdness! The hair dyed so black it's purple. And the accents, God bless the accents. My friend Julie, from Foodline, ventilated in that Long Island brogue that oozes superiority; I could have listened for hours, which was good because that's how long she held court. I began to scan subway cars for teenage girls, for the opportunity to catch a classic Rosie Perez. On such fortuitous occasions, it was important to sit near them, rather than stand, in case swooning ensued.

Oh these New Yawkers! They're brash and gauche, and they don't give a *flip* which direction the dessert spoon faces. I think I'm in love. I wanted to stay. Despite the bruises, I wasn't ready to quit.

So I shrugged my shoulders and soldiered on. After removing the glass from my wrist, and promising the theater I wouldn't sue, I picked up some temp work for a financial organization in one of the World Trade Center towers. Or maybe it was an insurance company. I honestly don't remember because (a) I didn't write in my journal and (b) a few weeks later it ceased to exist. Poof.

I was not stationed in its offices, however, but in those of the acquired business a few blocks away. My job was to transfer information from the defunct firm's paper files to a digital Excel spreadsheet. Excluding myself and one other temp, a shy wiry fellow who introduced me to Blimpie, the floor was vacant. Most employees had been laid off; the rest were now in the tower. So, naturally, I set up shop in the former CEO's expansive corner office, two full walls of which were glass, affording me a 180-degree view of Manhattan's southern tip and the waters beyond.

Wow. So this was the dream—to sit dozens of stories above the melee, above flatbed-truck galleries and snow-obscured grates. This office was the princess that the Cartoon Assassin protected so fiercely. This is why rookies flood the streets year after year, outrunning poisonous beetles: to get this view, and a private bathroom. Everyone in New York is racing to the bathroom in the sky.

Even though I was literally paid to work there, I had no business sitting at that palatial desk. It was probably made of mahogany or marble. It was probably handcrafted by bald eagles. It had never before held atop its sturdy frame the second half of a Blimpie tuna fish and banana pepper sandwich, which filled the room with fragrance because its owner hoped to stretch one $2.99 special through dinner.

I had warped. Through my own volition, and honest means, I'd reached world 2. But then, somewhere on that board, I squatted into a green tunnel that spat me out at world 8. It's fun to skip ahead, but warping is a dangerous tactic. Winning the game requires firepower and extra lives, and I'd arrived miniature and low on coins. Sure, my tuna fish and I were sitting on a cloud, but clouds can't carry weight.

A few days later, we fell through. On a Tuesday morning, I overslept and woke, with the rest of the world, to a real assassin, a true exhibitionist, one whose work appeared live on my living-room television.

When the towers fell, so did every New Yorker simultaneously. Gravity found us the way consciousness does when you're trying to dream. And we slapped the ground hard. We lay there for a while, a couple of days maybe, like a human blanket, some kind of last-resort barricade between the sky and the earth.

And then we stood slowly, brushed the sand from our clothes. The game had been paused. The screen was no longer rushing past, thrusting us relentlessly forward. So the players looked around, wandered in every direction, and began the long process of checking in, of sharing in the burden of proof of being all right.

Gorilla? Gorilla?

Gorilla? Gorilla?

My senseless, self-centered notions of New York life went up in the dust of everything else, the pulverized steel and glass that, no longer erect, followed the whim of the wind, heading to TriBeCa, the East Village, and across the East River, where it blew through open Brooklyn windows, landed on sofas, and embedded itself in the bare legs of those who'd been miles away. It covered us in a toxic patina. We combed it through our hair and breathed it in our lungs, tracked it indoors and hung it in our coat closets, this gruesome reminder that matter had not been destroyed but merely changed shape.

How arrogant I had been to think the city was out to get me.

I was so accustomed to living in a petri dish back home, that I self-indulgently invented an all-seeing scientist in New York. But the reason I was having a hard time here is because, guess what?, life is hard in New York. That I could be daft to something so obvious illustrates how easily I'd gotten by before. I'd never realized that the Southern villagers who watched were also protecting.

Although my cell-phone radar was jammed, my friends and family reached me that Tuesday. In my computer were dozens of e-mails. Everyone wanted to know everything about everyone. Word was delivered to my Luddite parents, and then, through a sprawling train of reply-all e-mails, my college friends began to account for all of our pals in the city, some of whom are still being sought.

When New York restored cell service, Aunt Jane's call was the first to come through:

"Please come home. Something else could happen. It's dangerous. Come back and stay with me, where I can keep you safe."

It doesn't make much sense, but after discovering a nonfictional threat, I no longer felt threatened. He's not an all-powerful wizard. He's a criminal. And even though Aunt Jane could never have imagined to warn me about this, she'd still delivered the advice I needed: Don't look at him.

It's true that one cannot fight New York, but the reason is that New York won't fight back, and therefore we remain invincible. We ain't studyin' you. It's inefficient. That had been a hellish wave—it knocked us over, stole our breath, dragged us through the sand and blinded us with salt—which can mean only one thing: Another will surely be hot on its heels. The best we can do is stand up, shake the water from our ears, and face forward. North Carolina may be the village that reared me, but New York is the one where I was raised.

Bid Day in Brooklyn

As children, we are taught that the seemingly pointless lessons of grade school, however menial or inscrutable, are actually preparations for travails later in life. Relay drills in soccer taught me to work with others. Geometry gave me the tools to shape an indefinable world into usable terms. And, thanks to Mrs. Palmer, my dry-mouthed, ninth-grade English teacher, I am acutely aware of when white balls of spittle collect in the corners of my lips.

I abandoned this philosophy in college, when faced with a trial so pointless and trivial, it couldn't possibly have had an adult counterpart. It was Rush, the week I visited a dozen sorority houses, selling myself at each. But I was wrong. It does have a real-world doppelgänger: the rooms/shared board for New York on Craigslist

.org. Both are facilities designed to help people find places to live. Both aim to pair you with like-minded individuals. In fact, the only difference between the two is that this time around, no one filmed the procedure for a commemorative video.

Most Craigslist ads seek gainfully employed tenants, so I conveniently and consistently failed to mention I was planning to quit my full-time job the following month. I knew I'd still be good for rent, so what did it matter? And the fact that I had a cat currently living at a boyfriend's apartment? It never came up.

I feel no shame; this sort of equivocation is part of the game, a game whose rules I learned in Rush. For example, at the Kappa house, which was known for having the highest GPA, I said, "I'm thinking about going premed." That wasn't a total lie. I *was* thinking about it...thinking that I wouldn't do it. And at A-D-Pi, whose ladies wore their hearts on their sleeves, I said, "Don't apologize, Courtney—if I'd just been singing in the candlelight with all of *my* 'sisters,' I'd be crying too." This wasn't a lie because I might very well blubber like a mascaraed fool in that situation—but since I knew I'd never *be* in that situation, the outcome was impossible to prove.

A week before I left for college, Tucker—one of my aforementioned elder and real sisters—knocked on my bedroom door. She headed straight for the closet. Tucker had also been through Rush at the University of North Carolina at Chapel Hill. As an expert, she'd promised to help me choose outfits appropriate for each house's style. It was like packing for a week of costume balls. "Chi-Os go out a lot, so wear something cute and trendy," she said, pulling from my closet a fitted top and a pair of black pants. "But the Pi Phis are more laid back; they smoke a lot of pot." Her interpretation of that was a flowery skirt and oversized white blouse. So, clearly my sister did *not* smoke pot. Then, she sashayed out of the room saying, "Just remember, the most important thing is to be yourself!"

This year I wore Marc Jacobs to meet the publicist in Brooklyn Heights and rode my skateboard—a skill learned in New York, mind you, not North Carolina—to the artist's pad in Bushwick, all the while playing up a different part of my varied past depending on who was listening. The girls in Boerum Hill wanted someone with a sense of humor, so they heard about my gig freelancing for *Saturday Night Live*. Since the guy in Chinatown worked at a hedge fund, I told him about my stint at a leveraged-buyout firm. One time, I misjudged. An ad agency associate ended up being more Goth than Madison Avenue and I spent the hour-long meeting obscuring my designer purse behind my pleated-pant legs. I am not proud of this behavior. But after living through four years of Rush—first you peddle yourself, then the house—I was working off instinct. The eighteen-year-old me was in the driver's seat. And she said, "I think I remember this from a kegger."

Still, no matter how hard the sell, someone has to buy. Craigslist, like Rush, is a popularity contest. Once, while leaving a particularly dreamy loft in Williamsburg, I ran into the next appointment coming in. Not only was she gorgeous and carrying architecture books but they already knew her! She was a legacy. Everyone knows that "legs" automatically get bids. I briefly considered pulling a Tonya Harding on her, perhaps by planting uncool contraband in her paint-speckled messenger bag...like a Goo Goo Dolls CD or *The Wall Street Journal*. Any sorority girl worth her weight in insignia T-shirts knows how to throw the competition off the scent of a nice young freshman. Sometimes the end justifies the means. But even this srat-brat has her moral limits. So, as the current roommates greeted her with hugs and "How's Greg doing?"s, I did nothing but take one last look at the exposed-brick bedroom that would have been mine. Good-bye, sweet, sunlit oasis two blocks from the subway.

There were other times when it became clear that my Craigslist suitors would dump me pre-U-Haul. While chatting on a couch in Cobble Hill, I watched one roommate make eye contact with another and roll her eyes. She'd broken the cardinal rule: Never reveal your true opinions about a prospect *to* the prospect. It's much more polite to do so behind her back. Perhaps, for example, when her picture pops up on the wall during a pre-Rush slideshow presentation of incoming freshmen. This little multimedia gab session is, of course, kept secret from the prospects themselves. Then, along with the rest of the seedy side of Rush, it's revealed to each pledge class when the girls return their second year to work the system from the other side. "I'm so glad I didn't know any of this when *I* was going through," Tri Delt sophomores could be heard saying during various phases of the process.

We required Rushees to attach photographs of themselves to the applications they mailed in before arriving. Then, via a grade-school-style projector, we threw the snapshots one by one onto the white lunchroom wall. If and when you knew the girl whose image appeared, you were instructed to describe her with only three adjectives. (With approximately four hundred pictures to file through, the system relies on brevity.) Such descriptions usually went like this: "Outgoing, academic and...and...beautiful on the inside *and* out!!" Now, even those for whom English is a second language will recognize that the third adjective in that series is actually one adjective, two adverbs, a preposition, a conjunction, and a defining article, all of which ultimately add up to *two* adjectives, giving the speaker a total of four. Still, the infraction was repeatedly allowed. And each time, I imagined particularly pulchritudinous intestines.

The use of whole sentences, however, was explicitly forbidden. Still, that did not stop Susan Barrow from standing, when Joan Wimberly's Polaroid shot on the wall, and saying, "Yeah, I know her; she slept with every guy at our high school." This was followed naturally by a few gasps, after which someone else said, "Well, I certainly don't want to eat lunch next to a slut." *That* would be the time when, whispered from somewhere in the darkness, a gentle voice could be heard: "I'm glad I didn't know about this when I was going through." Such a statement implied, depending on who heard it, that the speaker was either one of the few sane people in the room or was a slut herself.

Once the Rushees arrived at the Tri Delt house in the flesh, sisters could no longer talk about a girl behind her back. It would have been too risky. So we did so behind *our* backs. We used a secret body-language code to signify when a prospect was particularly difficult to talk to. Perhaps she was extremely shy. Or had belligerently accused us of caring what girls' fathers did for a living. Or had mentioned her dad was a plumber. Regardless, I was never allowed to leave my keep unattended, so my instructions were to smile sweetly and, while asking one more time what her major was, make a fist with my right hand and place it firmly in the small of my back.

"May Day! May Day! SOS!!" The small gesture spoke volumes. Within seconds, a "floater"—the girl whose job it is to troll for back fists—would appear. She aided in the conversation, made sure the poor freshman was having a good time, and ensured she'd still want to be one of us even though the use of the back fist had already secured her a spot on our C list. This is probably what happened to poor slutty Joan, who was no doubt greeted with a rousing hello when she arrived, in spite of the fact that it had already been silently decided she'd never get a bid. Joan would have been hugged, entertained, and invited to partake of the queso nacho feast available in the back house—a tactic designed to find out if, in addition to being a slut, she was also a heifer.

Food is typically available during the open houses of Craigslist apartments too. It's almost always cheese, fruit, and crackers—to be specific, Brie, white grapes, and Wheat Thins. I'm still not sure what it is about this selection that unanimously screams, "Welcome to our home!" Perhaps it is a way of proving that the area bodegas sell more than Slim Jims, white onions, and beer.

Sometimes there is also red wine, but it was usually gone by the time I arrived, the purple-stained lips and teeth of my hosts betraying who'd consumed the lion's share. I could forgive the transgression. Running through a Rolodex of vapid questions with strangers is not fun. It's a discomfort akin to watching Andy Rooney on *60 Minutes:* not painful per se, just boring and insulting to my intelligence. Therefore, having to do this with twelve people—in a row—would be like spending an entire Saturday in Andy Rooney's home while he cleans out his bathroom cabinets. And that is enough to send even the sanest to drink. I understood my hosts' desire for social lubricant; during each of the three years I Rushed freshmen, I kept a bottle of vodka under a friend's bed inside the house.

From the other side, whether as a prospective pledge or tenant, there is one relief far more profound than alcohol: a trip to the bathroom, the one room in the house or apartment where I could be alone and sit in silence for at least three minutes without drawing suspicion. It was rare that I actually needed to use the room for its intended purpose; I'd seen the insides of several others that day. But hosts were never the wiser. During these dubious respites, I understood the word "restroom" as anything other than a euphemism. While searching for an apartment, I also used these rests to script the perfect closing statement. Leave them wanting more, right? Be so charming that when the door clicks behind you, they say only nice things—because you can be sure there will be categorical judgment.

In Tri Delt, we used note cards and the numbers one, two, or three. In the ten minutes between the time one round of Rushees left and another arrived, each member of the house was to grade every girl she'd met. In what remained of the ten minutes after the house was cleaned, the plates restocked, and the decorations fixed, each of us was to sum up an entire person's worth—based on five minutes of conversation—and distill her talents, history, idiosyncrasies, and endeavors into one number. One number of three. Not big fans of gray area, these sororities. I wasn't sure how it would specifically work with New York lease holders, but I knew the effect and intention had to be basically the same.

And so I found myself standing in the bathroom of an affordable, spacious four-bedroom in south Greenpoint, carefully considering how I'd say good-bye, when I noticed a trinket on a shelf by the sink: a purple candle in the shape of a pansy. Normally, chintsy candles don't betray anything about their owners beyond a misguided taste in interior design. But this one was different. The pansy is one of Tri Delt's symbols. It's upward-facing bud represents optimism and a hope for the future. The pansy is the third status—or third delta, if you will—of sisterhood: *alumnus*. I leaned in for a closer look and, sure enough, discovered three small triangles etched into the tiny statue's wax base. Someone in that apartment had been a Tri Delt. And she openly admitted it.

My fears were confirmed when I returned to the living room to find one of my hosts, the one wearing sweatpants with literature on the ass, holding a Polaroid camera. "Would you mind if we took a quick shot?" she asked. "We've just met so many people, you know; it really helps to put faces with names."

I couldn't believe it. I would be in another multimedia gab session. How foolish I'd been to think I'd met my last. How much I wished I'd never met any. I thought of all the twentysomething girls who'd smiled for the same camera, unaware of what it meant, of how their images would be used. I would have killed for their blissful ignorance.

Of all the callous and catty ways to judge someone, using her picture is the worst because, although it happens behind a girl's back, she is also technically in the room. She's there, but helpless to defend herself. While her sense of worth is bluntly assessed, she smiles back without a clue, unmoving and optimistic. In her graduation gown or cheerleading uniform, wearing her yearbook best or prom dress, with her family at the beach, sitting in a mall with a Slurpie, standing next to a shiny new Volkswagen Jetta, at the top of Pikes Peak on a hiking trip. Her suntanned face smiles back, unfazed and unaware, like the mentally challenged kid in school who interprets your mocking as friendship.

Standing against the wall of that Brooklyn apartment—smiling, posing, pretending—I wondered what my three adjectives would be.

Like a wallet or a pair of sunglasses, I found my new home in the last place I looked. Again, I thought of Rush, during which each girl is assigned a counselor at the start of the week. The counselors are all in sororities, but remain anonymous so as not to sway the decision-making processes of those in their herd. Therefore, they are absolved of all duties within their own sororities. There are two ways one becomes a counselor. Either she requests the position because she is an enlightened woman who's already realized that Rush is insipid. Or she is nominated for the position by her house's Rush chair because she is deemed an embarrassment to the house. Perhaps she is geeky. Or overweight. Or has cankles.

When I was a freshman, my counselor said to our group, at least a dozen times, that we didn't need to worry about how to choose a house because as soon as we walked inside the right one, we'd know it. It would speak to us.

This is categorically false. Sorority houses can't speak to anyone in particular because they have no individuality. At best, they're amalgamations of hundreds of women, and, at worst, creations of their national business offices. In effect, they all kind of feel the same—synthetic and affected. Therefore, anyone who claims to feel an instant bond either is lying or will end up working for Corporate.

So you can imagine my surprise when I discovered that what isn't true for sororities is on the nose for apartments. A New Yorker's home speaks volumes. The four-story walk-up littered with incense sticks hinted that my potential roommate didn't like to clean. The two-bedroom with sheets and blankets taped over its windows told me that its resident was either depressed or a vampire. And the inch of mold growing in the corner of the three dudes' shower mocked me for having considered that a man under the age of thirty would take responsibility for anything, ever.

Then, in the three-bedroom, third-floor walk-up in north Greenpoint, I knew. Real-estate lightning struck. When Mary met me at the door, I thought, *I like her dress. And her hair.* Then I realized that she looked exactly like me. So at the same time I found a home, I also discovered that I'm narcissistic. The place was clean, cheap, and not too far from my office. And then, without taking a photo, offering me nachos, or stealing an inquisitive glance at the girth of my ankles, she offered me the room. I said yes, realizing that this time around I wouldn't be forced to chug a bottle of Boone's Farm the night I moved in. I know; I was disappointed too.

The First

Eff-You

I should have anticipated a fight. Traveling strains relationships. During long journeys through foreign country, animosities brew and small disagreements flare into full-fledged fisticuffs. And ours had been a long and taxing journey indeed: We'd been on Staten Island for three hours.

My friend Morgan organized the trip as a destination birthday party. She called it "an exploration" and posted a call for crew members over Evite. The first item on the itinerary, after we were to arrive on the island: "6:30 p.m.: Drop anchor and plant flags in new territory. Commence conquering of natives."

She promised to provide streamers and tissues for our loved ones during the bon voyage "from the Manhattan port of call." She told us not to worry about communication as her friend Annemarie spoke "Islandese." She explained that we wouldn't come home until we'd concluded "the spreading of smallpox."

Like proper pirates, we prepared for our work by drinking. Blessedly, the Staten Island Ferry sells beer. Unless you're a commuter, and sometimes if you are, boozing is the paramount reason to ride. On a Saturday afternoon, the experiential combination of sun, wind, and buzz eclipses even the stunning views of Lady Liberty. She may as well have said, "Give us your poor, your hungry, your weekend warriors."

Once on the island, the drinking continued. By the time we'd settled in at the second destination on our journey, a curiously empty saloon on Hylan Boulevard, we were good and toasted. I *really* should have seen it coming.

While standing by the bar in the saloon, someone in the party said, "This was my last borough. I've hit them all now. I guess I'm finally a New Yorker."

And then Jake snorted. "Bullshit," he said, wiping the underside of his nose.

"Why?" asked the befuddled offender.

"First of all," Jake explained, "this doesn't count as a trip to Staten Island."

At this point, I agreed with his argument, if not his bullish method. In spite of the fact that we'd eaten with local families at an old-school Italian restaurant, and would soon be rubbing groins with local teens in a terrifyingly loud, underwater-themed dance club called Atlantis, this didn't feel like an authentic trip to Staten Island—perhaps because we referred to these locals as "natives." Our journey was, by design, ironic. We didn't have fun; we had "fun." We kept enough of a distance that it was impossible to tell whether the wax spiking the teenage boys' hair was manufactured by Goody or Madame Tussaud.

To their credit, the locals just as obviously gawked at us: a clan of buttoned-up twentysomethings who referred to themselves as the Blogerati. I know what that word means, yet I still don't really know. It would also be an appropriate title for tiny gnomes who clean castle moats.

So did the circumstances of our trip warrant the checking off of Staten Island from the list of boroughs visited? Jake seemed to argue that dancing inside an oceanic nightclub—just so you can say you did—does not. And when compared to truly authentic Staten Island visits, such as meeting a new boyfriend's parents or identifying a body, it was difficult to argue otherwise.

"Furthermore," Jake bloviated, "visiting all of the boroughs is *not* what makes you a New Yorker."

He paused momentarily, waiting for someone to ask, "What does?" However, so impatient was he to play the pedant, he continued before anyone had the chance. "You're only a New Yorker after you've told a stranger to fuck off." He accented the last word by sucking air through his teeth.

In that case, Jake must be the New Yorkiest of us all: He'd already blessed out a car on Hyman for failing to light its headlamps, taken a shot at a too-bold seagull in the ferry terminal, and assaulted the end of a beer for growing warm. Put off as much by him as his point, I rolled my eyes and mumbled, "Here we go."

Jake shot back: "Yes?"

"Well, I mean, come on" I said, "plenty of people in this city get by without shouting obscenities."

"And I'm saying that those people aren't truly New Yorkers."

"That's too narrow a—"

"Why? Because you've never done it?" he interrupted.

"Done what?" I stalled.

"You've never shouted 'fuck you' to a total stranger."

I quickly scanned the street scuffles from my past, but the answer was already clear to us both.

"No," I admitted.

"Then you're not a New Yorker," he said, raising one eyebrow and slightly cocking his head toward the other, a movement that caused one dribble of sweat to swim precariously from forehead to nose so that when he self-satisfactorily pulled his glass of whiskey to his partially curled lips, I was able to pray that the perspiration would drip into his drink.

"Well, that definition works for you," I said out loud. *Because you're an aggressive asshole,* I said in my head.

Walking around accosting one another: what a self-destructive way to behave! It always escalates. If Jake had been piloting the *Titanic,* he would have claimed that the iceberg nudged him first.

And, besides, it's ridiculous to argue that there could only be one answer to the question "When does one become a New Yorker?" There are as many answers as there are people living in the city. It's a very popular topic of conversation. No matter how varied their origins or social statuses, every naturalized New Yorker has, at one point or another, entertained the question. However, depending on who you are, your response might be, "The first time I got mugged" or "The first time I mugged someone."

When the bodega owner knows how you like your coffee.

When you leave the city and get carsick from all the driving.

After your first conversation across a subway platform.

When you learn to like to eat alone.

The first time you're captured in the background of a tourist's photo.

The first time you picnic in Central Park and *don't* feel like you're in a movie.

Although there are certainly other universally encountered questions in New York, for example, "Spare some change?" and "What are you looking at?" there is no other that elicits such a variety of answers—not even, "Who's your favorite cat in *Cats*?"

"Putting aside the unbridled aggression thing for a minute," I said, this time using my vocal cords, "how can you even argue that one definition could apply to everyone in this city? I know the subway really well; you could drop me anywhere and I'd find my way home. That makes me feel like a New Yorker. But there are people on the Upper East Side who've never *been* in the subway. Are you telling me that means they aren't New Yorkers?"

"Of course that's not what I'm saying," he boasted. "Just the other day, I was told to fuck off by a dude in a suit getting out of a limo."

Arguing with him was like shouting at deaf people, or more specifically at my deaf cat, as she is also very annoying.

"You're implying that these belligerent New Yorkers had never accosted strangers *before* they moved here. And, furthermore, that people in other places around the globe *don't* scream at strangers."

"New Yorkers are born in other parts of the world every minute," he countered. "Sadly, some of them never get here."

So being a New Yorker is like being a preop transexual? That idea is preposterous—although, it did seem true in his case, as he was acting like a superfluous dick.

"What about people who were born here?" I asked. "Surely there are some who've never had this 'Eff-you moment'."

"Being born in New York does not necessarily make you a New Yorker," he said. "There are more people in the city who weren't born here than who were. Native New Yorkers are a minority. Therefore, based on the numbers, being born here cannot necessarily define you as a New Yorker."

He'd made this argument before; it was well rehearsed. What infuriated me was that much of it made sense.

"Look," he sighed. "You know I'm right; you're only fighting me because you've never done it."

"No, I honestly believe—"

"Where are you from?" he interrupted.

"North Carolina, but I don't see what—"

"Southern: typical."

"What?"

"You people are very passive-aggressive."

"Well, geez!" I said, before sighing audibly, crossing my legs, and looking the other way.

"Exactly," he snarled.

It's true. I've littered countless squares of innocent sidewalk with furious mutterings intended for my aggressors. Some of the things I've said to concrete include, "Maybe *you* should get out of the road," "Maybe *you're* blocking the stairs," and, my personal favorite, "Oh yeah? Well. *Yeah!*" Zingers, all of them, eh? I really showed that crosswalk who's boss.

I never fight back. Ever. Not once have I returned a verbal assault hurled at me on the streets of New York. Yet I am doomed to remember them all. My brain keeps a perverse catalog, and there's one in particular that's never on back order. Every time I see an overweight, baseball-capped man with a beard—which is pretty frequently in New York—I cower slightly out of muscle memory. While crossing an intersection in Hell's Kitchen our shoulders bumped and he yelled, "Watch where you're going!" I stopped, and pulled my head out of my book just in time to make eye contact as he spat, "Stupid bitch!"

OK, I realize that this specific collision was my fault. I also know that, generally, people who read while walking are a special breed of bothersome (I'd grown cocky with the whole hive-brain thing). Still: "Stupid bitch"? He said it with ferocity and intention. The slur was not thoughtless; it was not tossed off. He aimed before he shot; he hit me in the gut and it hurt. So I said, "I'm not a bitch, I'm...I'm a human being!" which is the most cowardly response possible. But, then, of course, I had no reason to be ashamed as I didn't actually say it out loud.

What a wounded little princess I am, so dumbstruck by the staggering injustices of brutish goombahs. I shouldn't care. He certainly didn't: Two seconds later he was whistling. And I was—oh God, it's embarrassing—crying. Walking along West Forty-Fourth Street crying, asking the sidewalk for justice. "Why did he have to be so mean? Where does he get off? Who gave him the right?" But the sidewalk did not answer; I suspect it couldn't hear me through the gum.

I try to recall my mother's directive in situations like this. If, for example, the woman at the U-Save-It checkout counter had been rude, Mom would smile even wider at her and then say, after we left, "You know, she's probably having a bad day, bless her heart." But try as I might to cull that sympathy, all I could muster was, "I *hope* he's having a bad day!" I was angry: mad enough to stamp my foot, to slam a door. I was so mad, I could have typed in all caps. I felt my face flush. People were staring. My inner response? "See what you made me do? You...stinky-poo!"

I whispered to myself on Forty-Fourth Street, "Let it roll off your back: Be the duck, be the duck." Be the duck? Like the one in old paintings who's in the mouth of a Labrador retriever? And anyway, if I'd really let the altercation roll off my back, I wouldn't remember it so clearly now. Instead, it seeped through my gossamer-thin skin, planted seeds, and blossomed into full-fledged hatred—which also remained inside me.

I've never fought with a friend. I've never fought with a boy-friend, not even during breakups. I think the last time I screamed at anyone was in boarding school. One afternoon, while hanging out with several other girls in Alice Lute's dorm room, I got overly excited about some topic—I don't remember what, but I'm sure it was nerdy. Alice rolled her eyes and said, "Gah, Jane, *calm down!*" When you're a spaz, and have spent your whole life being a spaz, you grow very sensitive to those two words and to their judgmental implication, "You are embarrassing me." It is one of the few things in life that can send me from zero to sixty in an instant.

I shouted at Alice, "I will *not* calm down!" and then I left, a move that effectively fulfilled her request, considering an absent person is as calm as they come. Thirty seconds later, at the other end of the hallway, still fuming, it dawned on me that the box of Hot Tamales I'd just purchased at the student store was still sitting on her floor. I have lamented the loss of that candy for years.

The bottom line is, I'm completely inept at fighting. Discussions I can nail. But as soon as things get heated, I'm all stutters and tears. I grow irrational and everything comes out wrong. Then I pout, say "That's not fair!" and run away. Be the duck? Obviously the bird I've chosen is ostrich.

So no, my yellow nature was not news to me. But I hadn't before considered that such passive-aggressive tendencies might be related to my origin of birth. And when I thought about it, Jake's theory made sense. Of course my skin is thin: It's completely bereft of scar tissue. If strangers bump into each other in the town where I was reared, the fighting they do is over who can apologize first.

Years ago, Aunt Jane and Uncle Lucius were invited to a cocktail party in Raleigh. At the last minute, my aunt changed her mind. She wasn't sick; she just didn't feel like attending. But she couldn't fathom insulting the host by canceling. So, instead, she convinced my uncle to go alone—and pretend she was there. Throughout the night, when someone asked, "Where's Jane?" he'd say, "In the living room," or "By the hors d'oeuvres," or "You just missed her; she went to the bar." It was a large party and, as she figured, no one noticed. The following morning, my aunt called to thank her host, telling her it was lovely to see her. She also received a few calls herself, from friends complimenting her on the previous evening's ensemble. Apparently the emperor *was* wearing clothes, and they were "divine."

This is how docile my childhood environment was—all of the time. In polite Southern society, there are no natural predators. We're a gentle island species that has never known aggression due to an absence of wildcats. The South is like the Galápagos Islands. How ironic that so many people there think Darwin is bunk.

So I guess, before I was the ostrich, I was the big dumb blue-footed booby. I waddled around New York looking to make friends with everyone because I'd never been taught to fear. Hello, shivering man in the oily hooded sweatshirt! Want to come home and meet my mom?

I might not be a fighter, but give me some credit; at least I am no longer a boob. One learns quickly in New York. Allow me to recognize a few of my tutors.

MAN 1: [*Holds door open.*]

JANE: [*Smiles widely.*] Thank you. [*Walks past.*]

MAN 1: Damn, girl, look at that ass.

MAN 2: Excuse me, does this train stop at Park Avenue?

JANE: [*Smiles widely.*] Well, it stops at Lexington, but Park is just one...

MAN 2: Cause I want to "park" myself in that ass.

MAN 3: [*Stares from corner.*]
JANE: [*Thinks*, I know where this is going. *Chooses
to avoid eyes and look downward instead.
Instantly realizes her mistake.*]
MAN 3: [*Masturbating.*] Aaaassssssss.

That last time was the day the booby's bird brain grew three sizes. I came to understand the notion of predators—and that I am *prey*. I'm not ashamed to admit it: I am afraid! If that goombah's first comment made me cry, imagine how damaging his follow-up. It's not passive-aggressive; it's just passive. I'll throw objections and epithets at the sidewalk instead. As opponents, we're a much better match.

Here's what I don't understand, though: If people in the South have found a way to be nice to one another all of the time, why can't we can achieve that in NYC?

Hilariously ideological or not, I said as much to Jake. His reaction to my naïveté is best described as spit-take.

"Oh please!" he spewed, whiskey dribbling from his mouth. "Everyone's nice in the South? What a crock of bullshit! They just wait till you leave the room. What's that saying you have down there? 'Kill 'em with kindness'? *Y'all* may use a different weapon, but the intention is the same."

Ack. Aargh! The sweaty drunk guy was *right*. I couldn't stand it. It was like the one time I agreed with a Christopher Hitchens article. Fine, yes: Sometimes Southerners say "ugly" things behind one another's backs. But you know what? If that goombah had waited to call me a "bitch" until later when he was hanging out with his girlfriends over iced tea, then I wouldn't have cried all the way down West Forty-Fourth Street. What did he achieve by hurting my feelings? It didn't teach me a lesson about reading while I walk; if anything, it cemented my proclivity to do so as a tiny silent F-U, which is, again, the most passive-aggressive way I possibly could have reacted.

"Besides," Jake continued, "of course you can be nice to each other in the South: No one is ever pushed to the limit!"

He's never seen my mother on Christmas Eve.

"Each person has, like, a hundred square feet of personal space to, I don't know, play banjo in," he said. "There are more than eight million people in New York! When you're crammed together, tensions build—exploding is how we reestablish stasis. It's the natural order of things. The sooner you accept it, the better."

I don't want to accept it. I refuse to believe that when Billy Joel said he was in a New York state of mind, he meant he felt like punching a cabbie.

"But general public politeness *has* existed in New York," I said. "Recently! In the weeks after 9/11, everyone went out of their way—"

"Ah, 9/11," he said. "I thought you might play that card: typical."

Typical! Typical! He was making me crazy.

"Well, it's true," I persevered calmly. "And the same thing happened during—"

"The blackout?"

No wonder strangers scream at this guy.

The point I would have made, had I not been interrupted by the splattering of his self-righteous spittle on my cheek, is that in the aftermath of the attacks on the World Trade Center, for at least two weeks, the air was empty: No car horns honked, no construction workers whistled, no bike messengers crashed.

But you already know this; I wrote about it in a previous chapter when, because I was typing instead of arguing, I could articulate the ideas and represent them via an egregious repetition of the word "gorilla." To him, though, I was unable to explain my experience of watching two people approach a one-lane stretch of sidewalk and then, instead of racing to beat each other through, they both slowed and invited the other to pass.

And, yes, it was a slippery slope. After those few weeks, we quickly fell back into bad habits. Regardless of all the flag and T-shirt reminders of our claim that we never would, it didn't take us long to forget.

"The point is: it happened," I said, "proving that it *is* possible— in New York City—for the baseline of social interaction to be unselfish."

"Car wrecks *happen*! Is 'slammed into a tree' the natural state for an automobile? Don't get me wrong: I think it was amazing how the city pulled together after 9/11. But it was an aberration— that is all. I don't wish for the natural state of play in New York to be belligerent, but there's nothing I can do about it. That's simply how it is."

"Of course there's something you can do about it!" I shouted, alarming the other members of our party who slowly made their escape to the back of the bar. "Stop perpetuating the system! Stop acting like a jerk. But you don't want to. You want to believe that the city is naturally belligerent, because that justifies your own aggressive behavior. It makes you feel better about being a bad egg."

He started laughing. Oh God, I thought: I called him a "bad egg." When would I stop proving his point about me? I felt like a butterfly tacked in a box.

"Well, well," he mocked. "Someone's getting angry."

"No I'm not," I said, though my bottom lip betrayed me.

"Yeah you are. And you know what? One day you're gonna explode," he said.

"I don't think so."

"Everyone has a breaking point," he persisted. "Everyone in New York will eventually break. And so will you. One day you're gonna pop and go all Bernie Goetz on someone."

Bernie Goetz? As in, the "Subway Vigilante," who shot four thugs on a 2 train? Now it was my turn to say, "Typical!" (But, of course, I didn't.) Why do New Yorkers love to romanticize violence? I'm surprised we haven't erected a statue of Travis Bickle next to Lady Liberty. To me, the nuts with guns are the aberration in New York. But, then, obviously I want to believe that—for the same reason I accused Jake of wanting to believe they're the norm. Labeling them perverted helps me justify my yellow-bellied nature.

Which is why the notion that I might emulate Goetz was preposterous. When I'm pushed against a wall, I don't shoot; I try to blend in with the paint. These boots are made for running, and possibly leaving behind cinnamon-flavored candy as a gift.

At the same time, though, I do have friends in New York—reasonable, polite Southerners—who *have* gone all Goetz, who somehow crossed over. I know because, so shocked were they by the incidents, they talked. Carter, from Greensboro, North Carolina, hawked a loogie on a taxicab when it cut him off in the street. Tiffany, from Charlotte, told a group of teenagers on the subway to "Shut up!" And Abbie, also from Charlotte, once confessed that, after being struck in the face by the briefcase of a man running up the stairs, she turned and screamed, "Fuck you!" Each story was followed by something along the lines of, "I don't know where it came from" or "I'd never done anything like it before."

So, terror upon terror, what if one day I flip out on some poor girl reading a book while she crosses the street? If so, does that mean

I'll also be fat and unattractive? Plus, if Jake is right about that, is he also right that that's when I become a New Yorker? And if that's the case, then where the hell had I been for the last five years?

It's true that living in New York can leave one feeling invisible. The city is indifferent. And you are but one in the sky of eight million stars. It can compel you to act like a child, to shout, stamp, and punch to get attention, to prove you actually exist. Maybe howling at each other is like planting a flag in the soil or carving your name in a tree for next season's campers: It's just another way of saying "I wuz here."

And then it dawned on me. I thought about the goombah and my mom's words: "He's probably just having a bad day." Feeling so ignored that you doubt your own existence is—on a scale of 1 to 10, with "bad hair" being 1—a really bad day indeed. I tried to feel for him.

That girl reading the book just bumped into me. What, did she not see me? Am I invisible? Oh God…what if I am invisible! Am I a ghost?!? Quick, think: What did I have for breakfast? I can't remember! Did I even wake up or have I just been wandering Hell's Kitchen since the moment I died? How can I find out? I know: "Stupid bitch!" Hooray, she heard me. And she's crying—oh, thank God.

So maybe Jake was on to something, even if for a different reason than he'd thought: When you have been forced to question your existence to the point that you need to prove you're alive, you become a New Yorker. Cogito ergo sum a New Yorker.

Or maybe that goombah just thought I was a bitch. I don't know now, and I certainly didn't that night on Staten Island. So instead I responded to Jake's Goetz comment by saying something like, "You're a douchebag."

Erm, that came out wrong.

"Good one, Jane. Look: I'm tired of talking about this. You know I'm right; you're only arguing because you hate being a coward."

"No: What I'm saying is—"

He stood up and motioned toward the rest of our friends by the bar. "Come on, guys. Club Atlantis calls."

Wait. I wasn't finished with him. It's like he wasn't hearing me. It's like I was making no sound. It's like I wasn't even sitting there.

"So you're just gonna walk away," I said.

"Jane, *calm down.*"

I felt the blood rising to my face. I stood up from my barstool, stuck my finger in his face, and said, "Fine: You know what, Jake? *Fuck you!* Is that what you wanted? Does that make you happy?"

It did. His lips curved into a most sinister smile. And even though he wasn't a stranger, we both knew he'd won.

The skies didn't open up; there was no ticker-tape parade. I felt no different. Actually, I felt a little nauseated, but I think that was the Italian food. I also felt a little ashamed. And then I hiccuped.

Jake stood. He reached for his jacket with one arm, threw his other over my shoulder, and said, "Come on, Bernie, let's discover Atlantis."

Long after we'd left the bar, I suspect his smile remained.

Sink

Staring a Gift
Horse in the Mouth

Aunt Jane didn't want to mail the present to my office. But I can't receive packages at home. "You still don't live in a doorman building?" she asked incredulously. "Is that safe?!" This question—along with any relating to my lack of security, wedding ring, or blond highlights—is followed by the cry "Hoahhh!" a dramatic half moan designed to convey that she is concerned and, mostly, that she thinks I should be too.

However, before eliciting a noise of such volume, she pulls the phone slightly away from her mouth in consideration of the listener's ears. Because even in fits of hysteria, my aunt, a Virginian by birth and North Carolinian by address, is a lady. And that, as it turned out, is exactly why I received a package. During a recent trip home, she'd spied certain aberrations in the polished behavior I was taught as a child. She'd noticed what I hadn't: Since moving to New York my decorum has atrophied. I'm a lapsing Southern Belle. This package was her way of pulling me back on to the wagon.

"Oh. My. God." I said, staring into the box lying open on my keyboard. "It's a manners book." This nugget of information pulled two or three of my coworkers from their desks.

"No way," Adam squealed, grabbing the thin, hot-pink hard cover and reading its title, "*How to Be a Lady: A Contemporary Guide to Common Courtesy*." That nugget attracted a few more neighbors.

"It gets better," I said to my growing audience. "Parts have been highlighted in pink."

As a proper Southern child, I learned a specific code of wisdom widely recognized as "etiquette." Some of its edicts are intuitive and commonplace. For example, it's impolite to chew with your mouth open. The courteous nature of this is unarguable. No one should witness the marriage of ham biscuit and collard greens in midmastication. No one should have to answer the question, "Do you like 'see food'?"

Other directives are more abstruse. Once, while helping my mother refill the candelabra on our dining room table, I watched, puzzled, as she lit each candlestick several hours before dinner.

"Why are you doing that?" I asked.

"Sweetie, you *never* display a candle with a fresh wick," she responded. "Now help me blow these out."

"What's wrong with a fresh wick?" I prodded.

"It's tacky."

"Why?"

"It just is."

"But *why*?!" Her impenetrable logic had reduced me to the

five-year-old who responds to every answer with another question.
There had to be a reason! Unless you take the Moses story literally,
rules don't fall out of the sky. They have origins. Maybe, in feudal
times, I wondered, a host preburned candles as a way of proving to
his guests that the wax wouldn't emit a poisonous gas. Or maybe,
at some point in history, kerosene lamps became a hallmark of the
lower class so if one had real wax candles, he wanted his guests to
know it. Or maybe one time Jackie O lit hers by mistake and told the
Vanity Fair reporter, "I totally meant to do that."

I asked again and again until my mother finally said, sternly and
exasperatedly, "I don't know, Jane . . . it's just *what you do.*" And that,
of course, is the most accurate explanation I could have received. To
truly understand etiquette is to take it without question—because
the real answer is itself impolite and therefore verboten by the same
code being questioned. That circular truth is this: One follows the
rules of mannered society in order to prove she knows them.

Although there are general guidebooks, such as the one I
received in the mail, information regarding the more obscure end of
the etiquette canon is exclusive to oral history. The extent of your
knowledge is a résumé of how well you were reared, which reflects
directly on your parents' worth. Each time my sisters and I left our
home, we were on display and accordingly assessed. Every meal,
shopping trip, church outing, and car pool was a recital. Growing
up, I was watched as if by a hawk, except without the eventual relief
of being eaten.

Once, while I was setting the kitchen table—a full spate of sil-
verware at each place, even if we were only having stew—my mother
answered the phone.

"Hello, Pam!"

I knew instantly that Mrs. Andrews had called to report on our
chance encounter that afternoon at the Hop-In convenience store.

Like a perfect soldier, I'd walked her out to her Mercedes, carried her purchases, opened her door, and capped off the exchange with, "See you Sunday in church!"

"What beautiful manners she has!" I heard Mrs. Andrews's voice crackling through the receiver. "You've done a wonderful job." Mom beamed. I didn't tell her that I was really just occupying the woman's attention so my friend Kristen could buy us cigarettes.

Regardless of the motivations behind the actions, I'd followed the code. And, like I said, the code matters most. In the big city, though, people follow a different set of rules, which is to say, they don't. New Yorkers are nice, mind you; the rude stereotype is largely false. But we don't do anything for the sole purpose of *doing it*. Although we live within a few miles of both the Statue of Liberty and the Empire State Building, most of us have visited neither. In other words, we don't even do things with well-established purposes. Pointless endeavors never had a fighting chance.

This neglect of niceties can be disconcerting to visitors. It was for my friend Wortley. She lives in Wilson, a small eastern North Carolina town, which is actually pronounced "Wiltson" (I think this is where all of the silent *t*'s go). To give you a little context, Wortley and her husband, her cousin and her cousin's husband, and her parents all live on the same street. I don't even know the name of the person in the apartment across the hall.

Wortley and I went shopping in SoHo. Afterward, I hailed us a cab, requested our destination, reclined in my seat, and launched back into the conversation we'd started on the street.

"Jane!" she said in shock. I was being scolded, but I didn't know why. She threw her Theory bag on the floor, leaned forward, stuck her sun-freckled nose through the small crack in the partition, and said, "I'm sorry, sir. How are *you* today?"

Point taken.

"I wasn't being rude," I heard myself saying a little too defensively. "I was respecting his space. Surely he wants to be left alone." But my blustering was wasted; Wortley and I had both seen him smile in the rearview mirror. The jig was up. Chastened, I explained that the curt nature of New Yorkers—careful to distance myself from the group—shouldn't be interpreted as rudeness. It's a side effect of being so busy; it's symptomatic of having to deal with the sheer number of other people in the fishbowl.

These excuses hold water, but they aren't the whole story. There are fundamental reasons why a culture of etiquette will never grow in Gotham. First, manners require social interaction while New Yorkers are bred for anonymity, naturally selected to blend in and go unnoticed. Those who accidentally stand out get mugged. Or, worse, end up on reality-TV prank shows. Neither does one want to be mistaken for the kind of person who *intentionally* stands out, for example, evangelical Christians or, worse, actors on reality-TV prank shows. Otherwise, a New Yorker moves silently through the city like a preoccupied ghost. That's why we wear black: the better to disappear.

Another reason mannered society won't thrive in New York is because its dwellers—excluding those in a small subsection to the east of Central Park—share a suspicion of the upper class and, by extension, exclusive societies. It's a unifying aesthetic. We all fear that, at any given moment, the draft riots will break out again and we'll be on the wrong side of an angry mob.

Gawker.com could only have been born in New York: While the rest of America worships celebrities, New Yorkers worship those who mock them.

For example, my college roommates, most of whom now live

near one another in the Triangle area of North Carolina, visit each other frequently—at book clubs, the country club. Among them are memberships to garden clubs, bridge clubs, the Junior League, the Terpsichoreans, Daughters of the American Revolution, and the Colonial Dames. I, meanwhile, share groceries with a few others in the office to save money and suddenly am the target of malicious derision. When coworkers pass the kitchen as we chop broccoli, they sneer sarcastically, "Oooohhh, it's the *lunch club*! I wasn't invited. I guess I'm not good enough to be part of the *lunch club*— boo hoo hoo!" Other words I've been told were used behind my back: "precious," "exclusive," "obnoxious," "stupid," and "twee." Raw cabbage and a can of beans are twee? Maybe in a Charles Dickens novel.

The point is, no one in New York wants to be a part of your stupid club.

It didn't take long for this sentiment to rub off on me. My mom says I've turned into a "reverse snob," which cuts me to the quick—not because she's wrong, but because, by categorizing me as its opposite, she still defines me on a snob's terms.

This is not to say that New Yorkers don't exercise common courtesies. Even the crudest thug will give his subway seat to a pregnant woman. But he didn't learn to do so from his parents—the rule is printed on a poster on the subway wall. Mayor Bloomberg thought it was rude to blow smoke in the faces of strangers, so he passed legislation banning cigarettes in public places. Up here, the manners we exercise are simply called laws. And the ramifications of the NYPD justice system are far more painful than being cut from the Hawthornes' Christmas-card list.

But laws, of course, are an extension of "necessity," a word you will never find in a manners book (unless it's been grossly misused). Then again, the plush world of my youth embraces a different understanding of needs: In addition to oxygen, water, food, and shelter, the list also includes decorative soaps shaped like their owner's dog. Such superfluities are the blessings of a good life. Unfortunately, they don't travel well. For example, if Aunt Jane finds her food bland, and spies a shaker on the other side of her husband, she will not ask, "Lucius, will you pass the salt?" Instead, she asks, "Lucius, will you have some salt?"

"No thank you," he responds. "Will you have some salt?"

"Yes, please. Thank you," she says. And he passes it to her.

That's the rule: You always offer whatever you want to someone else first. But in order to get it back, the other person has to know the routine. If Aunt Jane moved to New York, she'd become known as that strange lady who offered everyone seasonings. She'd either have to give up salt or carry some in her purse.

People up here don't understand niceties; anything extraneous is suspected of betraying an ulterior motive. Once, when I called a coworker's mother "ma'am," she responded, "Are you buttering me up?" Other responses I've heard to "ma'am" include "I'm not that old" and "Do I look like I run a brothel?" Eventually I broke the habit; actually I've shattered more than a few. That means when I go home, I have to pull my manners out of storage, slip out of my rented ghost costume, zip on a great big smile, and recalibrate the tenor of my voice to say with gusto, "Hey y'all!"

This is a bit dishonest, but it's best to keep the ins and outs of my heretical city life a secret. My family has visited me here, but they've never been inside my apartment. If they want to believe that I own a single piece of furniture that wasn't found on the street, let them. If I happen to innocently buttress that fallacy, it's just because I was reared right. White lies are incredibly polite.

Sometimes, though, while juggling my two sets of social mores, I drop a ball. I forget to place my fork and knife toward ten o'clock to signify I'm finished eating. I forget to rip off a bite of bread *before* I butter it. I forget that burps aren't acknowledged with fist bumps. Mix-ups such as these are how I came to receive a gentle reminder in the mail. The hawk eye of my aunt misses nothing.

Adam stood by my desk and flipped through the pages of *How to Be a Lady* with greedy laughter. He is not an obsequious person. He's an overworked, underpaid theater critic who finds his only solace in the free dinners occasionally offered to him at cabaret clubs. A summation of his worldview: after the cater-waiters at an art event noticed Adam stalking them, they launched a campaign of avoidance, rushing past him with trays held high above their heads, to which Adam responded by giving chase and then returning to me with a mouthful of mini crab cakes, saying, "They expect me to have shame."

He landed on a page at random, pointed to a highlighted passage, and read, in his best Blanche DuBois, "A lady never adjusts her bra or bustline within view of other people."

Then he paused, shifted his countenance, and said sympathetically, "Oh, Jane, sweetheart—you actually do that a lot."

What? No I don't. I mean, the wires are uncomfortable. And no bra ever truly fits. So sure, sometimes I might reposition a boob here or there just to make sure everything's in order and—oh, crap; I *do* do that a lot. I guess it hadn't occurred to me that anyone would notice...that I was digging my thumbs into the sides of my breasts and tugging at them?!? Of course they notice! Duh: If I'm not looking at you, you can still see me. Hearing Adam say as much out loud was like finally hearing the answer to that riddle about the guy who killed two hundred people when he turned off a light. Duh: He works in a lighthouse. Not only does it make perfect sense, I can't believe I didn't think of it before. What next? Are you gonna tell me that I Can't Believe It's Not Butter isn't butter?

I had been prepared to dismiss my aunt's gesture outright. But now it held water. What other nasty habits was I *not* getting away with? How far from the flock had I strayed? I told Adam and the rest in our peanut gallery to buzz off, and then I stashed the book in my messenger bag so I could pore over it later in private.

How to Be a Lady is a loosely organized collection of one- to two-line maxims: "A lady does this," "A lady does not do that." The words "should" or "might" do not appear. The author, Ms. Candace Simpson-Giles, offers edicts, not suggestions. Her text is law. It *was* brought down from Mount Sinai, probably in a tasteful leather valise.

The directions and admonishments follow, one after another, in a long mechanical list. So many rules and regulations! So much to remember! Does Ms. Simpson-Giles really follow all of these? How could she get anything done if constantly preoccupied by the way to do it? I imagine her spinning one way and the other in sensible slacks until her hard drive overrides and she puts the mop in the oven and cleans the floor with a green-bean casserole.

Rules. Pshaw! I've always had a problem with authority. During a recent Thanksgiving dinner, Mom and I got into a disagreement regarding whether or not she'd told me which trivet on the table was for the succotash. Then she turned to the crowded dining room and announced with a smile, "I swear, Jane would argue with Jesus!" Well, sure, if he chastised me for forgetting where to put the loaves and fishes when he'd in fact never told me, then yes, I would.

But right now I'll just argue with Ms. Simpson-Giles. Herewith, an open debate regarding certain excerpts of text my aunt decided should match their book's hot-pink jacket.

*A lady uses her best china or dinnerware
to serve her guests.*

To define a set of plates as "best" presupposes I own more than one set, which presupposes I have somewhere to store them. I have one set of plates. Because, like most people in New York, I only have two kitchen cabinets. And one of them is where I keep my bong.

*A lady always sets the table before
her guests arrive.*

Again, this assumes you *have* a table. Next.

*If something breaks, a lady is not
disturbed and does not allow her guests to
feel any guilt over the matter.*

I agree wholeheartedly. As my father used to say, "No use crying over spilled milk." Still, my mettle in this department has never truly been tested, as my dinnerware is literally valueless. When I say "literally" I don't mean "figuratively." I mean it was all free. My plates, bowls, and cutlery are a mishmash of dishes left behind by the dozen or so roommates who've moved in and out of my life over the years. My drinking glasses are either promotional items I swiped from work, which bear a variety of liquor company and hotel emblems, or they are Pom tea containers, the mason jars of my generation. As my mom says, "My name is Jimmy; I'll take what you gimme."

So, no, it doesn't bother me to throw shards of any of these things in the bin, as they were all, at one point in their histories, trash already. Besides, if something breaks at one of my parties, I'm usually the one who did it. Because I've usually imbibed the most. Hosting is stressful. Any lady will tell you that.

If a lady must excuse herself from the dinner table, she simply says, "Excuse me." No further explanation is necessary.

Tell that to my friend Will Hines. While we were out at a bar one night, I gave delicacy a chance; I pushed my chair away from the table and said only, "Excuse me."

Will, in a knee-jerk reaction to the information vacuum, looked up and asked, "Where are you going?"

Great, now I had the full attention of the table and two

decisions: (1) share my scatological pursuit far more openly than if I'd simply said, from the beginning, "I'm going to the bathroom," or (2) say nothing and walk away, which will naturally lead my friends to assume I'm either a dine-and-dasher, a member of the CIA, or a superhero—because any of those explanations is more logical than the notion that I had to relieve myself, considering that, had that been the case, I surely would have said so at the start.

I'm not suggesting you should clink your glass, stand, and shout, "No reason for alarm! Please carry on while I go pull my skirt up and"—well, you know what you'd shout. That I don't want to type it is why we created euphemisms in the first place. The word "bathroom" doesn't have anything to do with what goes on in there. There is no bath in most restrooms; neither does one rest there, especially not if you have to squat. These words allow us to be polite while still relaying important information, such as the answer to the entirely warranted question, "Where in the hell are you going?!"

But "bathroom" is still too much for my mother, who finally relented to my argument by saying, "Fine, if you must say anything at all, say you're going to *visit* the *ladies' room.*" No! You can't go around creating new euphemisms for ones still in perfectly good use.

A lady never places her napkin back on the table until she is finished with her meal and is about to leave.

I'd be willing to follow this rule if everyone else would. Instead, when I return from a "jaunt" to the "womyn's den," I find that my napkin has been taken off my chair, thrown open, refolded, and placed next to my plate. This is a problem because the sole purpose of the napkin is to get dirty so my clothes don't. If someone refolds it, I won't know which side had pea soup on it and which side was clean, which is especially a concern if I'm wearing white sometime between but not before or after Memorial and Labor Days.

At this point, I must hold the cloth up to the light emanating from the table's one candle and inspect it for stains. I find no instructions regarding this behavior in Ms. Simpson-Giles book, but I assume it's unacceptable.

Therefore, I've developed a way to buck the system. When entering an upscale joint, I make a point to notice how the linens are folded and where on the table they're placed. Then, on the occasion I need to excuse myself, I fold my napkin and leave it just so to dupe the waiter into thinking he's fixed it already. At this point I am free to leave the table without fear of dirtying my clothes upon returning from ducking out on the bill, assassinating a head of state, or saving a baby from a runaway train.

*A lady knows when to wear a slip or
half-slip and does so.*

A desire to hit home this particular nugget is, I suspect, what sparked my aunt to embark upon the post office—enabled literary lesson in which I'm currently mired. On that afore-mentioned trip home, I found myself in need of a slip—and without one.

I grew up Presbyterian. My family still goes to services. When at home, I do too. And the frock I'd packed for the occasion was clinging to my leg with truly religious fervor. Anyone walking behind me could have made out the holy trinity.

"Darling, just wear a slip," my aunt said. After a bit of silence, she turned back to me and asked, "You *do* have one?"

In truth, I had, and still have, several. A long black one, a short gray one. Pure white and sheer nude. I have some with slits, some with lace, and several that are far too big. Over the years, my aunt has given me each. "Do you need another slip? I'll get you another slip. Don't you want to pick out a slip? You can always use another slip." Even though they take up an entire dresser drawer, I can't bear to throw any away because you can always use another slip.

I had not, however, brought any home. "I didn't think to pack one," I told her. "Because I never wear them in New York," I said. "Because I don't wear the kind of clothes which require them," I explained. "Because I don't go to church."

OK, I didn't say any of that.

Instead, I said, "Shoot! I forgot to pack my slip. If you have an extra, that'd be marvelous." Throw it on the pile.

A lady wears hosiery to formal weddings and dinners.

I can't figure out how hosiery manufacturers stay in business. No one under sixty-five wears hose. And women over sixty-five probably get a discount. The only other hosiery-wearing segment of our population I can think of is drag queens. But only 11 percent of the population is gay, and only half of these are men, and less than half of this group likes to sing onstage. I suppose film-set designers occasionally purchase hose to hang over clotheslines in fictional shantytowns... but that could only be, at most, a couple hundred pairs a year. And there are also the pairs that criminals pull over their heads before robbing quickie-marts, but those are shoplifted anyway.

I won't pretend to have investigated the causes behind the cultural shift away from panty hose, but I imagine it has something to do with the word "panty."

A lady realizes that the purse she carries makes a statement about her.

Agreed. For example, the fading tie-dyed canvas bag on the shoulder of the fifty-seven-year-old with wild hair says, "I'm too tired to fight the establishment anymore." And the brand-new, multipocketed backpack on the clean-cut older man says, "I'm a pedophile." But I suspect Ms. Simpson-Giles's admonition reaches beyond general aesthetics; usually the statement made by a woman's purse is a *written* one, such as "Louis Vuitton" or "Kate Spade." Additionally, each of those written statements says one of two other things: either "I need you to know I have money" or "I need you to think I have money."

OK, Mom's right: I'm a reverse snob. But if there's anything

I learned during the two years I spent busting Chinatown counterfeiters, it's that the only statement a fake bag makes is, "I flew in from Omaha and all I got was this shitty bag!" (Hmm, sounds like I might be a good old-fashioned regular snob too. That would explain the self-loathing.)

All I want is to avoid making any statements, period. I would chalk this up to New Yorkification, but really it's a lesson I learned in college. If you are wise enough to recognize that, although that subculture gets the most press, most young black men are *not* gangsters, then you must also admit, no matter how prejudiced you are, that not all sorority girls are idiots. It's just that the ones who get the most press—who advertise their sisterhood via T-shirts, emblem baseball caps, and lettered pendants—are *exclusively* idiots. In college, they gave the rest of us a bad name. They made it impossible for me to wear any of my own Tri Delt T-shirts because, thanks to them, those letters made their own statement: "Date-rape me."

That lesson stuck. Ever since, when I receive a designer bag or wallet from my mother or aunt, I painstakingly remove the label before carrying it. I can appreciate the make and look of a purse without needing the world to know who's responsible for it. And yes, I realize this means the only difference between me and that fifty-seven-year-old with the wild hair is that I have slightly better taste. But I'll tell you this: I bet she never got date-raped either.

When a lady pours from a bottle of wine, she finishes by turning the bottle slightly upward, thus preventing drips that might stain.

Um, I know this one already. Not because I'm a lady. Because I'm a wino. Unless those are the same thing, in which case I am way ahead of the curve.

A lady is mindful of her appearance at all times.

Like the bit about the slip, this highlighted entry is more than a general suggestion. My aunt is making a specific behavioral critique. Since I've been old enough to wear makeup (let's say fifteen; that is, JonBenét was *not* old enough) my aunt has been begging me to do so. "Darling, don't you want to put on a touch of lipstick?" "What about some mascara?" "How about a little rooooouge?"

Over the years, I've fired back with several logical traps. "Are you saying I *need* makeup?" to which she dutifully responds that of course I'm beautiful without it but "imagine how much prettier you *could* be."

Usually some mention of "You never know when you're going to meet a man" is thrown in, at which point I counterattack with, "The guys I like prefer women who don't hide behind a mask." That usually gets me a "Hooooaahh!" in Doppler effect as she huffs out of the room.

My disdain for cosmetics stems from many sources, but I'll mention just one. My roommate in boarding school wouldn't leave our dorm without several layers. To visit the commons area, to get frozen yogurt off campus, no matter where we went, we first had to wait while she applied what she called her "daily confidence." I don't need to explain why that's twisted.

To be honest, though, I'm mostly just lazy. It takes ten minutes to apply the stuff in the morning, plus an extra ten throughout the day to touch up, and another five to remove it at night. I could use that time to exercise, which will do far more for my appearance than lipstick. And if I end up spending those accumulated twenty-five minutes watching bad reality TV instead...well, there's nothing in Ms. Simpon-Giles's book about motivation.

When a lady makes her way down a row in a crowded theater, she faces the people who are already in their seats. A lady never forces others to stare at her backside.

So instead I force them to stare at my crotch? While, at the same time, bumping my rear into the unsuspecting heads of those sitting in front of us? This makes no sense at all. Does the maxim also apply to church pews? Because then, the one who'd be forced to stare at my backside is Jesus. And if his job is to judge the quick and the dead, I don't want him assessing the size of my ass.

In truth, neither option is sound. Whether you enter facing forward or backward, those already seated will be indisposed. That is why, when faced with a crowded row, I seek out a peopleless route. Typically, this involves finding an empty row one or two away from mine, walking down to the middle of it, and then crawling over seats until I reach my own. No one is disturbed and I get some exercise: win win.

A lady knows that whenever there is doubt about the color, black is best.

Here, here!!

A lady uses the word "companion" when introducing two friends who live together. She realizes the term denotes a special relationship that is beyond boyfriend/girlfriend.

Actually, "companion" means gay. So if by "special relationship," you mean "gay," then yes. Otherwise, the word "companion" is off-limits...at least until gay marriage is legalized and we can all use "husband" and "wife." That's the rule so don't confuse people. If you introduce me to a woman and say that her partner is by the buffet, I will assume this partner is also a woman. Then, when her boyfriend returns with a plate of food and sits next to me, chances are I'll hit on him. Believe me, she won't be more inclined to forgive the transgression when I say, "Sorry, I thought you were gay."

*A lady is not ashamed to ask for the
sexual history of a man with whom she
may become intimate.*

I can't believe she highlighted that. No one in my family has ever talked to me about sex. I'm not even allowed to use the words "stink" or "snot" under my parents' roof; it goes without saying that no one's uttered "erection" or "secretion." My sisters and I don't even broach the subject with one another and we're all over thirty.

This is officially the most awkward way a family member has ever brought up the birds and the bees—fifteen years too late and via a pink highlighted passage in an etiquette book. Which means, I guess, that I've got to hand it to both my aunt and Ms. Simpson-Giles for proactive intentions. Still, it's important to note that my aunt did *not* highlight the piece of text directly following that passage: "A lady is not ashamed to purchase condoms or other forms of birth control." I guess in some ways it's still a man's world.

I don't get joy out of this battle; it doesn't please me to discount Ms. Simpson-Giles's edicts. In matters of etiquette, I do need help. I want help. But this book, although claiming to be contemporary, offers little guidance regarding the situations of my modern New York life. Perhaps she simply forgot those chapters, so I'll pose my questions now in case she's reading.

When I'm out and about, is it unladylike to use a store's bathroom when I don't intend to buy anything?

If I'm feeling too lazy to do dishes, is it more mannered to leave them in the sink for my roommate or to take bites directly from her block of cheese and return it to the fridge bearing teeth marks?

If I'm throwing a party and I run out of glasses, is it more ladylike to force my guests to drink out of common paper cups or to pass around the bottle saying, "Most of you have made out with each other at some point anyway?"

I called my aunt that night to thank her for the package. "You opened it at work, didn't you?" she asked.

"Yes."

"Hoahhh!"

"I'm sorry," I said before realizing she was holding the phone away from her face and couldn't hear me.

I hadn't intentionally gone against her wishes. I just found her request dubious. My aunt sends packages all the time: a pastel reversible raincoat, a paisley-print shower cap, a bag full of eye shadows. I don't complain. I love the presents. I've gotten a lot of slips out of the bargain. So how was I to know this package would be so different and sensational as to truly require secrecy? On my part, as Condoleezza Rice once said, it was a lack of imagination.

Besides, I couldn't rob my coworkers of the opportunity to see the parcel's contents. They've come to appreciate these packages— hers are the gifts that keep giving. One time a box landed on my chair while I was out to lunch. When I returned, my desk mate Erin had already checked the return address and spread word throughout our pod: "Jane's proper aunt sent another one." They are fascinated not only by the contents, but even the wrapping: shiny white paper, a pale-green cloth ribbon (of which she says all her friends are jealous), and one large sprig of rosemary tied into the knot (because "Rosemary is for remembrance").

"Why is there a plant on it?" Erin once asked.

It's like receiving artifacts from an archaeological dig. Which piece of cultural ephemera would it be this time? "Ah, Professor, your hypothesis was correct: Southerners *will* monogram anything."

Obviously my aunt didn't know any of this—yet somehow she still knew it.

"Your New York friends might think I'm silly," she said, with eerie accuracy. "But listen to me, Jane: You are *not* from New York!"

Ain't that the truth. The more time I spend here, the more it sinks in. Or rather, the further I get from North Carolina, the stranger my home appears. What I'd thought was reality turns out to be a specific anomaly.

You mean people in other parts of the world don't give each other sausage for Christmas? Every year, for decades, their children don't wrap forty to fifty tubes of raw pork in red and green paper, affix "Love, the Bordens" tags to their twisty-ties, and deliver them around town? Occasionally, if it was a family's first time on our list, or if a new housekeeper answered the door, the bags of raw meat were accidentally placed under the trees. On Christmas morning, they became, to unsuspecting children, a surprise far more disturbing than the truth about Santa.

I thought celebrating Christmas with pork was completely normal. Being disabused of this notion suddenly threw everything else into question. What else had I been taking for granted? The deli on Sixth Avenue that accidentally gave me unsweetened tea? After which I made a mental note that up here one must *specify* sweet instead of assuming it understood? "Guess what," I told myself. "That place probably doesn't sell sweet tea at all." Furthermore, I bet—regardless of the window sign—it *isn't* the "Best Deli in the World."

And what about that restaurant on Thirty-Sixth Street? The barbecue spot that *happens* to be owned by Koreans? Like how sometimes Chinese people own taco shops? It probably serves a different style of barbecue altogether that—dear Lord, deliver us—might not even be made out of pigs.

Eventually, of course, came the bigger realization: There are *so* many people who don't celebrate Christmas. When my friend Bartow received a copy of the office vacation calendar at his first job in New York, he asked a coworker, "Who is Rosh Hashanah?"

Growing up in Greensboro, I knew one Jewish girl. And her dad owned a jewelry store. But I didn't know that was a stereotype until recently. Because I didn't know anti-Semitism still existed until I moved to New York. Seriously. I knew it *used* to be a problem, but I thought it had been isolated and cured on D-Day like a strain of polio. Obviously, I was the isolated one. At least my ignorance was optimistic.

For this and other reasons, my life is the subject of wonder to New Yorkers, who sit elbow on knee, chin in hand, and wide-eyed while I talk about the thirty-seven cousins who crowd in my parents' living room every Thanksgiving, or the grocery store in Goldsboro dedicated solely to pig products (yes, there's an entire aisle of chitterlings). My Northern friends especially love the rare occasions when my flattened accent remembers its rounded lilt.

Once, while backstage at a comedy theater, Aunt Jane called my cell phone. It wasn't the best timing but our conversations are typically brief and one-sided. She runs through a litany of yes-and-no questions, tells me she loves me, and hangs up before I can say, "Good-b——." So I snuck into a quiet corner of the green room, turned my back to the crowd, and answered my phone.

"Yes ma'am.... Yes ma'am.... A pink sweater, black pants, and flats.... Yes ma'am.... Love you too.... And Uncle Lucius.... OK, by——.... Hello? Oh."

I closed my phone, spun around, and discovered a small audience.

"'Uncle *'Lucius'*?" my friend asked incredulously. "Lucius! Who were you talking to?"

"Um, my aunt," I replied. "In North Carolina."

"You sounded different," he said, and then imitated the drawn-out short-a in the way I'd said "Bye."

I tried to push my way through the crowd. "Wait," he pressed. "Did she ask what you were wearing?"

"Yeah," I said. "She likes to know that I look nice."

"But you *aren't* wearing black pants," my friend said pointedly. "You're wearing jeans."

What she doesn't know won't hurt her. Yes, it was a white lie, but I don't utilize them as frequently as people think Southerners do. Directly after divulging my roots, I often receive one of two responses: "People down there are *really* nice" or "People down there aren't *really* that nice." Since moving here I've had more than one person confess an initial dislike for me. For example, Brian Finkelstein. We knew each other for years before we became friends. Once, in passing, I asked, "How come it took so long?"

"Because I didn't like you," he said matter-of-factly.

"What?"

"I thought you were annoying."

"Wait—what?"

"Well...the enthusiasm; I assumed it was fake."

Nope: I'm honestly so optimistic it's cringe-inducing. I assume that, when he came around, his line of reasoning went, "She's still annoying, but at least it's sincere!" Or perhaps he read a copy of *How to Be a Lady,* as Candace Simpson-Giles clearly notes, "A lady knows that false congeniality is as obvious as bad false eyelashes."

Of all the colorful idiosyncrasies of my Southern life, none is as interesting to Yanks as the time my father paraded me around an auditorium in a poofy white dress like a prize heifer. I was a debutante. And no, I'm not embarrassed about it.

OK, I'm embarrassed about it. Therefore, a confession requires several follow-up exceptions and qualifications. For example, yes, I grew up with money; yes, I have a couple of sets of married second cousins; and yes, I was a little pudgy in high school . . . but I am not a snobby, inbred pig!

This is why, rather than repeat such a refrain, I typically hold the information until I *choose* to reveal it, for example, when someone else admits it first.

One day, I sat at the counter of Hope & Anchor in Red Hook, Brooklyn, anonymously enjoying far too many french fries, when I overheard a gentleman next to me telling his friend about "the strangest experience." The friend was enthralled, giddy and full of questions: "So they just walked around in a circle?"

"Yeah. Weird, right?"

"And they really wear white dresses?"

"Totally. Wedding gowns. And I had to wear a tux with tails."

It was so tempting. I wanted to trade stories, have a laugh. But I was unsure. I've been burned before. Northerners love to mock us. The stereotype is always the same: dumb, racist, and clinging to the past. Sometimes it doesn't matter how much you explain or contextualize information. When I told my friend Rachel what I mentioned earlier about not knowing that Jews still experienced racism until I came to New York, she responded angrily, "That's horrible; you shouldn't tell people that." So much for honesty.

But my Hope & Anchor neighbors seemed to face this "deb" experience with curiosity. The escort's friend had questions. He needed answers, information. And I needed someone to talk to between mouthfuls.

"Wait," his friend prodded him. "Dudes were in the ceremony too?"

"Oh yeah," I interjected, entering the scene like the mysterious stranger in the third act of a thriller. They paused and stared at me silently. I sloshed my soda for effect.

"Have you been to one?" the guy who'd been an escort asked with trepidation.

"I *did* one," I said. Then I swiveled around on my stool before adding, "Twice."

"Whoa," said the friend.

I was starting to feel like Robert Shaw's character in *Jaws* when he launches into the monologue about the sinking of the *Indianapolis*. "Eleven hundred men went into the water...Vessel went down in twelve minutes...Margaret forgot her mascara and had to borrow Leigh's!!"

They drilled me with questions. I told them about the choreography of the group dance and the duties of the "head deb." "No way!"'s were elicited. "Tell me about it"'s were exchanged.

And then, the question I'd expected from the start: "Why do people do it?"

I told them that, originally, the balls were a way for a father to sell his daughter into marriage; he presented her to society bachelors when she was of age. Hence the prize-heifer analogy. However, if you ask a member of a debutante committee today, the response will be, "To recognize families who've contributed to the community." Specifically, this refers to philanthropy, leadership, bringing business to the local economy, and so on. Ultimately, though, each family is wealthy—and, more important, has been for several generations. You know Matthew 19:24? The verse that goes, "It's easier for a camel to pass through the eye of a needle than for one who is rich to enter the kingdom of God"? In the South, they insert "nouveau" before "rich."

"But why did *you* do it?" the escort asked me.

I wish I could say it was because I was nineteen and didn't know any better. The truth is, the prospect of having a dozen parties and luncheons thrown in my honor was intoxicating. Also, did I mention the presents? So many presents. Why does one get gifts just for turning nineteen? I guess it's akin to receiving money at a bar or bat mitzvah, but as I believe I've made horrifyingly clear, I wouldn't know anything about that.

In answer to my new friend's question, though, there is no reason per se. There is no pragmatism or practicality. *It's just what you do.* I still harbor fantasies of one day encountering a situation that will call upon the skills I learned as a debutante and thereby retroactively justify my participation in the ritual. It would be my *Goonies* moment. The kids in that movie face a series of life-threatening challenges while trapped inside a booby-trap-laden underground maze. At one point, they meet an ancient piano made of bones and are instructed to play a sheet of music in order to pass. The character whose role up to this point was that of the whiny squeamish girl becomes the savior when she summons memories from music lessons past to accomplish the task. All I'm saying is, and I don't think it's too much to ask, it would be nice if one day a group of my friends and I could get kidnapped, right? And put in some basement where the walls are closing in. And then, just before we all get squashed, a disembodied voice says, "It's all over, kiddies . . . unless one of you can display a proper English curtsy!"

My aunt's displeasure over the manners-book incident eventually subsided and the deliveries resumed. By that point, her fame was officewide. She has a knack for building fame. People all over North Carolina and Virginia adore her for her beauty and charm and have spent my life telling me so.

"You're Jane Tucker's namesake, aren't you?" they exclaim upon hearing my name. "You know, she is a very fine·lady." Indeed, I do. Then they hug me and say that I must be wonderful too. That's some powerful runoff.

My aunt doesn't just greet you, she throws her arms up, fills her lungs with air, and then releases it by exalting your name skyward as if it's the answer to a quandary that had been stumping her for months: "Haaaaaaaaah, Jaaaaaaaaane!!!"

She refuses to admit how many marriage proposals she entertained in her youth, but my estimates put it at around four.

One of the afternoons she came to visit when I was a child, I remember hearing the click of her keys in the lock and running so fast through the back hall to meet her that my legs slipped and buckled under me like the overexcited dog that rams into a wall when it can't slow down. And she wasn't even carrying french fries.

Recently, I bumped into my friend Hobby, who lives in New York but grew up around the corner from my aunt. She grabbed me by the shoulders, locked eyes with me, and said, "I love your aunt Jane."

"I know," I said with a smile. "Isn't she great?"

"No, you don't understand." She pressed. "She gave me a

sixpence to wear in my shoe on my wedding day. A sixpence! I'll never forget it."

Whenever I talk to my college roommate, Katie, she asks about my aunt and says, "She always made feel like I was the most important person in the room."

This is especially true for me, her namesake. My aunt has no children of her own. When I visited her, growing up, I was treated like a princess. My parents' home is beautiful, I mean no disrespect, but they had to deal with three children constantly muddying it. Jane and Lucius's home was pristine. Anywhere you set your vision were trays of polished antique silver, hand-painted Herend figurines, perfectly fluffed pink and pale green embroidered pillows, and fresh-cut roses from her garden. She had almost a dozen varieties in her side yard—excluding one called 'Mr. Lincoln', which my grandmother said she couldn't plant because of "the War between the States"—and her friends would frequently pull in the driveway to admire them, particularly her favorite, a pink and white climbing rose named 'Eden' that had covered a stretch of white-brick wall five feet high and ten feet long.

Each morning after I stayed over, she made me a chickadee egg: one fried egg chopped with bacon and cubed bread, served in a tiny egg-shaped china bowl with delicate brown birds painted on it, and placed between a glass vase bearing a rosebud and a silver goblet filled with orange juice. I, meanwhile, was wearing a hypercolor T-shirt and growing out that bad perm.

Staying with my aunt also afforded me the rare opportunity of seeing her undone. She slept the way I imagined the Queen of England did, in a silk off-white gown that fell straight to the floor and felt like cream to touch. It was bordered with intricate lace, bore her monogram, and flowed when she walked like something you'd see in a Shakespeare production. I couldn't believe she looked that beautiful in the middle of the night. I imagined she dreamed about rolling prairies and fields of daffodils and never woke up tired. She said I was beautiful too. The brash ACC basketball insignia on my T-shirt argued otherwise, but I figured, Hey, I'm just a kid; my time will come.

When I slip off my Converse sneakers in my grubby Brooklyn apartment, shove them under the broken dresser I found on Franklin Street, and reach for a "Have a Guinness!" glass to fill with tap water, I realize that things didn't really turn out the way I'd planned—in spite of my aunt's subtle hints. That first post-book package she sent me? A polka-dot makeup bag. When I opened it at work, Erin parroted back to me, "Darling, how about a little rooooouge?" I laughed. She laughed. It was funny.

After that came a knee-length, pale-blue terrycloth sheath. It is short-sleeved, pulls over the head, has white trim, and, of course, bears my monogram. I'd never seen such a specimen before. Was it a day robe? An apron? I held it up for all to see. "I think it's the WASP version of a muumuu," Adam guessed. I laughed. He laughed. It was funny.

When the next package came, a couple of friends had already inspected the box by the time I got into the office. "Open it," Adam said. This time there was a card inside. She'd written, "I remember you used to love this." I dug into the tissue paper and pulled out the nightgown. It was a little more yellow than it used to be. And the lace had pulled away from the seam in a couple of places, but otherwise it was exactly the same, which is to say, resplendent.

"Ha! That looks like something out of *Flowers in the Attic*," Erin said. "Yeah, I think that's what Ophelia died in," Adam added. She laughed. He laughed. I got up to visit the ladies' room.

"Excuse me," I said, and took the garment with me.

Locking the door, I slumped onto the commode and started to

cry. The three-by-three stall was overwhelmed by the smell of my aunt's old house. After chemotherapy, she said it was too difficult to keep up all those rooms, so they opted out for a small condo. That was years earlier. The nightgown must have been stewing in a box since. When I closed my eyes, I could see the pale green sofas. I saw sunlight pouring through the breakfast-room window and glinting off the silver goblet. I saw a half-eaten chickadee egg and a green linen napkin with white trim, and through the screen door I saw her roses.

She tore out the garden before they moved. 'Queen Elizabeth', 'Peace', 'Tropicana', 'Just Joy', 'Double Delight', 'New Dawn'. She dug up each, giving the most vigorous to friends to replant, and leaving only one behind, the 'Eden' that covered her driveway wall. Unfortunately, it's struggling without her. The new owners have not been able to keep it strong. But the rosemary is thriving. Perhaps it remembers her. And so will I.

That was the last time I opened one of my aunt's gifts in public. Now I tote the traveling talismans home and inspect them away from Yankee eyes. Because, although it's true that I'm a New Yorker— Hoahhh!—I am *not* from here. I may wear a garish worn-out T-shirt during the day, but at night, I sleep like a queen.

Groundhog
Weekend

"She's a brick"—Mr. Haskins flung me out and spun me around—"house." Then he dipped me. And while horizontal, I had a premonition: an image of me sitting in mud next to a white tent. "She's mighty mighty." The next thing I knew, he was twirling me closer to the edge of the dance floor. "Just lettin' it all hang out." And although I now knew where this was headed, I was powerless to stop it.

Squish, squish, thump, sigh.

Those were the sounds of my pumps sticking in the mud in quick succession, my rear reacquainting itself with the ground, and me closing my eyes to suffer in solitude the indignity of the joke I instantly, also, foresaw: "Hey bartender!"—I mouthed along as Mr. Haskins guffawed—"Cut her off!"

I stared up at him and the white tent behind him, feeling dizzy and, yes, slightly buzzed, but mostly confused. Was I prescient? I had literally seen the future an instant before it happened, right down to the hackneyed joke. I felt like Cassandra at the ball, doomed to spout party-foul prophecies that old men won't believe. *No wonder I drink,* I thought, as the seat of my dress began to dampen with rain.

"Whoopsie Daisy," Mr. Haskins said, sticking out his hand. "Didn't see that coming, did you?"

Before I could roll my eyes, there flashed a familiar look in his, and everything made sense: I hadn't predicted the future; I'd relived the past. July, two years prior, Sea Island, Georgia. Different band, same song. Different friend's father, same extra-dance-floor tumble. Different couple getting married—same wedding, which is to say, of the Southern variety.

They're all the same. Sure, nuptial celebrations in general are pretty similar but, as I have come to realize since moving to New York and befriending people who invite me to weddings in other parts of the country, Southern people marry in a very specific way. And since one of those ways is in front of a huge audience—everyone is invited and everyone goes—I've experienced the Southern wedding many times, forty-one and counting by my best estimate. I relive the same weekend over and over and over and over and over again. It is permanently set on repeat in my life.

Sitting on the ground, looking up at Mr. Haskins, feeling the wetness soak through to my skin, I figured this out. It is a strange curse but I've used it to my advantage. Case in point: I have since danced many times in heels on a makeshift dance floor to the song "Brick House" by the Commodores, and I have since danced with the fathers of many of my friends, but never again have I landed in the mud. I'm doomed to repeat history, but that doesn't mean I can't learn from it.

As someone who has been afforded the knowledge gained from both repetition and comparison, allow me to enumerate the basic differentiating characteristics of the Southern wedding and, along the way, offer advice.

First and most important is the one I've already mentioned: size. There were 560 guests at one of my sisters' receptions and 430 at the other's—and those are only the people who came. Just so you know, years passed before my mother admitted how many people she'd invited to Lou's wedding (800) so yes, she realizes that some people find it strange. For Southerners, however, it is pretty normal. In fact, when faced with such high numbers, some brides find it easier to do away with lists altogether and instead invite the entire town. Literally. In small cities, including Tarboro and Washington, North Carolina, it is customary for a bride's family to print the reception's address in the local newspaper in lieu of mailing invitations.

Obviously there are small affairs in the South, but they are the exception. Small weddings are suspicious; they imply that the bride's family has something to hide . . . like a Yankee groom. So, in response to the exclamation New Yorkers most frequently utter regarding my summer calendar: No, actually, I'm *not* that popular.

Unlike in other parts of the country, a guest at a Southern wedding cannot give the couple money. It's considered tacky. After the honeymoon, they may return your present to the store and exchange it for money, but they first need a tangible gift to display at the bride's home. Old ladies will view the loot and gift cards remain attached, so your token of love had better be good.

Wear something pastel to the wedding-day brunch, especially if you're a dude. Men might also consider seersucker and bow ties, and if the luncheon is casual, remember that men wear shorts two extra inches above the knee in the South, and never wear socks with loafers. All of these style elements are part of a look that my friend Katie McElveen dubbed "Jethro-sexual."

The fourteen girls in matching outfits at the reception are not the entertainment; they're the bridesmaids. Six times have I been one among twelve or more. Sometimes there are honorary brides-maids, too, who were also friends with the bride in college but had been in a different sorority. Then there are readers, ushers, girls who pass out programs. I'm surprised there aren't also candle lighters, seat warmers, bag holders, aisle clearers.... Why not save money by bestowing on your friends the designation "bartender"?

I mock out of love. Yes, it is ridiculous to stuff twenty-eight people plus a couple and the preacher into the apse of a church. But it stems from a desire to be inclusive, which I find endearing, even if I'm out a couple extra hundred dollars because of it. Southerners want everyone to be a part of the celebration the way kindergarten teachers want everyone to participate in art hour. There is even a place for the kid who eats paint—which means, again, even though I have been a bridesmaid eight times, a junior bridesmaid three times, and an honorary bridesmaid once, I am *not* that popular.

Don't be shy at the buffet. The chicken fingers, deviled eggs, roast beef sandwiches, potato salad, shrimp cocktail, and tomato aspic are not the appetizers served during what people up north call cocktail hour. There is no cocktail hour. There is no sit-down din-ner. There is only buffet. Where would five hundred people sit? Right, yes: You'll probably have to eat that standing up.

Don't clink a fork to your glass. That is not the cue for the bride and groom to kiss, as it is in the North. If you clink, everyone will stop talking, turn around, look at you, and wait for a speech—which would be weird because toasts are done on Friday night during the elaborate pre-wedding-party wedding party, replete with another live band and buffet.

Don't ask about the "bachelorette party"; we call it a "girls' weekend." People aren't lined up to visit an electrical generator; that's actually a fancy three-room portalet. And don't expect the couple to be announced; it's considered tacky to draw attention to yourself in that way, so instead there will be fireworks when they leave.

Oh, and that pale bunch huddled by the bar wearing black? Those are the New Yorkers. They are friends of the bride from that year she spent getting a postgrad degree in partying New York style. They are discussing the town's quaint way of life. They are drinking vodka sodas and hitting on the cater-waiters. They can't believe that the men in this part of the country dance without dropping ecstasy first.

Now, I didn't fly all the way down to hang out with other New Yorkers, but occasionally I do flee to their dour corner, the way a kid runs to the safety of home base in a game of freeze tag. This is because, as long as I am with them, I am guaranteed not to have one of these conversations:

"So what you do for a living in New York?"
"I'm a writer."
"Oh, just like Carrie Bradshaw!"

"I hear you're writing a book."
"Yes, I'm really excited about it."
"Your ex-boyfriends must be getting nervous!"

"Is your book about trying to find love in New York City?"
"No. Actually, it's not. It's not about dating. Or sex. Or boys. At all. Not at all."
"Ahh, *I see.* It's about how you don't *need* men." [*Winks*] "You go girl!"

What? No! That...that's the same thing!!! Although I admire women who can write about their New York love lives, I am not one of them. But I can't expect people back home to understand this, because Sarah Jessica Parker ruined it for the rest of us.

Years after *Sex and the City* has been canceled, it still exerts its influence, spreads its myths. I am nothing like Carrie Bradshaw! First of all, I can't afford to live in Manhattan. Also: I have more than three friends, I do not squeal, my gay friends aren't bitchy, and this phrase has never been a part of my audible inner monologue: "I couldn't help but wonder....".

Regardless, again and again, I encounter people back home who imagine that my life in New York is spent pouting at rich men from inside a too tight, two-tone poof dress, which I will later stain with tears.

Aargh!

I wish I didn't know that experience so well, but it is part and parcel of being Southern-wedding omniscient. I have seen it all before. Whether you need to know about HBO-perpetuated stereotypes, or choreography as part of a cheerleading-squad-sized bridal party, I'm your gal. And let's be honest, you don't have a lot of other options. If you get an invitation to a rehearsal dinner party and the dress code is listed as "Delta casual," you can either come to me or hike through the Mississippi swamps seeking answers from an ancient shaman, because one thing is certain: You cannot ask the bride.

I began to experience these weekends as unique only after moving to New York, when home began to appear strange. Of course, most of the weddings I've attended have been during that period anyway—the postcollege period—twenty-eight of the forty-one, to be exact. That's a lot of plane flights.

In one particularly busy summer—weddings happen in waves, one of the many patterns noticeable from a macro view (another: the canonization of "Hey Ya")—I flew south for seven ceremonies. I was like a bird that couldn't grasp the fundamentals of migration. Whether on a sparrow's constitution or a girl's wallet, that is expensive behavior. So I picked up a second job waiting tables; this was that time I told you about, the summer I worked at Chumley's. When I revealed the aim of my enterprise to a coworker, her eyes grew twice their size.

"How many weddings?" she asked.

"Seven."

"In one summer?"

"Well," I said, "there are actually eight but two are the same weekend and, unfortunately, in different states."

"You mean you're *going* to all seven?" she stammered. "Couldn't you have said 'no' to some?"

I gave her a quizzical look. The inner question instigating my expression was: Why would I say no? But that did not come out of my mouth, for although I am slow enough to have never before considered that the "regretfully declines" option on a wedding invitation is in fact an option, I am quick enough to know that admitting such would betray too much. Instead, I uncrossed my eyes, made up an excuse that I needed to be home anyway over some of those weekends, and skillfully steered the conversation toward the flies.

"I know, *so gross,*" she replied and tottered off to seat some balding yuppies.

After that I did not broadcast my plans so liberally. It only raises questions, whose answers the interrogator would find insufficient. I was acting like one of those dogs that digs holes through the living room carpet: exhibiting a behavior beyond the borders of its correlating environment. This sort of disconnect would eventually have far-reaching consequences. Flying back and forth so frequently taxed more than my wallet; it turned me into a psychological mess. It would be difficult enough to oscillate between two different life-styles, but in my case, these lifestyles were both extremes.

Weddings are intense and euphoric, an amplification of a culture's best attributes. Think of the positive Southern stereotypes you know. Hospitable? Five hundred guests. Traditional? When the band plays beach music, my parents' generation crowds the floor with '60s era shagging. Colorful? There is a slightly senile woman in Wilmington, North Carolina, who invites herself to every local reception, and family after family only smiles and says, "Yes." Look for her next time you go; she'll be the one asking what sushi is.

New York is also an extreme—except it is that way *all the time.* This city is an amusement park: Everything is concrete, it's full of tourists, and food vendors line the sidewalks. It's like living in a casino: The lights never dim, there's an incessant din of bells and horns, and there's always someone, somewhere, crying in a bathroom.

What I'm saying is, a Southern wedding is like the South on heroin. And New York City is like *life* on crack. Therefore swinging between them rendered my brain a speedball.

There were so many behavioral changes to make with each transition, so many little things to remember! When I went home, I had to pack an alternate wardrobe in my bag, including elegant shoes, and a different vocabulary in my head, one with words such as "please" and "thank you." I had to learn to walk slowly. I had to learn to wait. Then, of course, two days later it'd be back to the city where people who "wait" meet the vocabulary *get out of the goddamn way,* and shoes are chosen based on their ability to step over those who didn't know in which direction "the goddamn" was.

At first, I screwed up. I'd bring home Chucks instead of heels and forget the difference between begonias and azaleas. I landed my proverbial rump in the mud on more than a few occasions. But this gave me an idea. Just as I'd done with the ins and outs of the weddings themselves, I would let repetition be my guide. If you experience an outcome frequently enough, you can memorize its preceding cues. Then, you will always know how you are supposed to behave. Yes, I realize that this is how sociopaths blend in. And that is exactly what I've been trying to tell you.

Here's how it works: If the woman at the checkout counter looks at me, smiles, and says, "Hot day out there, ain't it?" I am supposed to settle in for what might be a long conversation, even if there are people behind me in line.

However, if the woman at the checkout counter avoids eye contact, chews gum sullenly, and talks through me to the woman bagging groceries behind me, I'm supposed to continue texting.

Sometimes I must rely on tone. If the phrase "The body of Christ, the cup of salvation" is delivered monotonously, I eat the wafer and drink the grape juice because I am taking communion in my church back home. However, if the same phrase carries self-righteous judgment and aggression, I do nothing because I am riding the F train.

And if a woman asks, "How do you get around New York City in heels?" I know that I'm in the South, and also that I'm about to disappoint her. She wants me to respond by saying something like, "I take cabs" or "I carry flip-flops in my purse" or "Pain is the price of beauty, sweetheart." But all I can say is, "I *don't* wear heels." Because I am not Carrie Bradshaw!

The long manicured fingers of that show find and pinch me wherever I go:

"Do you go to all the hot restaurants?"

"Do you hang out with fashion designers?"

"Do you know anyone like Mr. Big?"

What? Are you kidding me?! The answers are no, no and...
well, sure, but so do you; charming narcissists exist everywhere.

I do hate to disappoint these women; their questions are an
act of kindness. They wish for me to lead a glamorous life. It's a
self-fulfilling optimism. They want me to be like Carrie Bradshaw,
so they assume I am.

And they want it for themselves. They imagine that if they'd
moved to New York, they'd live the *Sex and the City* life. Therefore
they need to live vicariously through someone who does, and that
person may as well be me. So...they couldn't help but wonder...
can't I at least do them the favor of occasionally drinking too many
cosmos and throwing myself at emotionally unavailable men?

Surely my days are spent dining next to celebrities, dashing in
and out of Diane von Furstenberg, and cutting velvet-rope lines,
because otherwise, why would I be in New York when I could be
home with them? By assuming the answer to this question, they
don't have to ask it. And I don't have to tell them otherwise.

Of all the tiny readjustments, however, of all the cultural altera-
tions necessary for me to pull off this constant back and forth, there
is one I cannot master: the volume of my voice. I leave New York for
the pastoral silence of North Carolina, crawl into a car or sit down
at the breakfast table, and wail. "WHAT CD IS THIS?" "WILL
YOU HAVE SOME SALT?" "WHY ARE YOU WINCING?"

I don't realize I'm roaring, of course, not even after I've heard
my own bellow. But then my patient mother covers her ears and I
apologize—in dulcet tones. Sometimes she even closes her eyes in
some synesthesia defense mechanism: "Please, Jane, you're screaming so loudly I can't see."

Still, fifteen minutes later I'm hollering again. Rinse and repeat.
Here's the disconnect: Although the background noise in New York
is prodigious, it is also omnipresent; I cannot perceive that I am

raising my voice to overcome it, because I do not recognize it's there. And I'm not talking about one's learned ability to tune out sirens or horns. There is a base-level, low-decibel constant buzz in New York that you *literally cannot hear.*

In an upstairs bedroom in my parents' house, one-third of my laptop's total speaker capacity is loud enough to enjoy music. Meanwhile, in my third-floor Brooklyn apartment, after midnight, when there are no screeching buses, screaming drunks, or cooking roommates, when, if I strain to listen I catch only occasional wind, full laptop volume is not even sufficient; external speakers are required.

Eight million whirring refrigerators add up to a whole lot of nothing. How voluminous this lack of volume! It astonishes me that a collection of sounds so large goes completely unnoticed, exists beneath the surface, affecting us in ways unknowable. It's like dark matter in space: We can't find the stuff but we know it's there because it alters gravity. Just like we only know "dark silence" exists because it turns New Yorkers into eighty-year-olds when they leave.

But in the city we do not know we're screaming. We merely aim to supersede the din. And then, in our collective ignorance of the sonic deluge, we slowly grow louder and louder until, eventually, no one hears anything but his or her voice. In the right place at the right time, you can yell bloody murder and disturb no one.

One night, after closing down a dive bar in Chelsea, my friend Shawn and I took to the streets with my iPod, one tinny earbud for him and one for me. As we reached Port Authority, Guided by Voices' "Glad Girls" came on and although we could hardly hear the music, or maybe because we couldn't, we sang—*"Hey, glad girls only want to get you high"*—and jumped in place and stamped our feet and wailed at the top of our lungs—*"In the light that passes through me."* The subway rumbled beneath, trucks bellowed beside, and no one could hear us scream.

This was my quintessential New York moment, standing next to a puddle of piss. So now you understand my reluctance to share such a defining motivation with my friends back home.

"Surely, Jane, the reason you've forsaken home for all these years is because your life in New York is fabulous. Right?"

"Nah, it's because in the middle of the night, in the part of town that smells like diarrhea, no one can hear you scream."

Who am I, hobo Freddy Krueger? Better not to say, not to let them know that I feel like a foreigner in what used to be my home.

And when I first moved to the city, it was the other way around! North Carolina was concrete, was reality. Therefore, New York felt strange: *It was the weirdest dream. I was in the West Village, and then all of a sudden I was on a train underground. And there was this guy talking on a cell phone—somehow, even though we were underground— except then he turned into a homeless guy . . . and the cell phone was actually a tin of mints . . . and the next thing I knew I was in Midtown! That's when I woke up.*

Then, during my urban tenure, a reversal: North Carolina became the alternate universe, the foreign land so peculiar it must be a dream. *So, we were in a car, right? Looking for a parking place. And the lot was enormous. It was like the biggest shopping center I've ever seen—but all of the stores were exactly the same. And we couldn't find a spot, so we just kept driving around and around in circles . . . endlessly. I remember thinking, Can't we just walk? And that's when I woke up.*

I no longer know which is terra firma and which incognito; neither can I choose which one I want. In all this back and forth, I constantly change my mind. Every time my plane touches ground down south, I breathe in air so thick with humidity and sweet with plant-produced oxygen, it feels like ingesting a cloud. People smile, and when they speak it sounds like singing. I become convinced that I must move back. But when my plane touches ground again at LaGuardia, my whole body buzzes with this electric Technicolor energy, the cars on the BQE look like they're dancing, and I'm all, like, *This cabbie and I are vibing on the same wave; we don't even need to speak.*

The distinction between home and destination has disappeared. I've lost my inner compass. I mistake up for down and contrary for contrariwise—I do not know which is the real world and which is the Looking Glass world where books are written backward and the sun shines at night.

It's as if each airplane is a passageway between two realms that are, to me, opposites, mirror images. And if that is the case, then every time I travel from one of my home/destinations to the other, the mirror image of me—the version of me that everyone at home thinks I am—must be traveling at the exact same time but in the opposite direction.

Oh dammit! I went and created the Carrie Bradshaw version of myself. I called the her-me into being. I should've left well enough alone. But it's too late now. She exists—and, boy, must she be disappointed every time she has to take my place in my crappy Brooklyn apartment with nowhere to fit her shoes.

While I'm toasting beautiful newlyweds in elegant clothes with expensive champagne, she's cleaning my deaf cat's litter box. While I party at fancy receptions into the wee hours of the morning, she sweats through the sheets because the air conditioner broke, she's trying to block out the souped-up stereo systems of teenage thugs.

And while I toil at my laptop, trying to write my way into understanding which life to choose, she clacks away on hers with confident clarity: *Men are like cities. Some will cook you dinner and spoon you to sleep; they're the hometowns, overweight in a cuddly way and always smiling. They're safe and dependable—but claustrophobic. They'll ask for a key to your apartment, come over while you're out, and then wait* up all night just to ask where you were. They'll always be there; they'll never change. And then there are the New Yorks, those bastards we chase like bad habits. They're charismatic and dashing and they never stay in on a Saturday night. They don't call and they don't sleep over; sometimes when you talk it's like they don't even hear you. But they leave you completely weak in the knees and just when you've sworn off them, they show up in a limo with flowers and tickets to the Met. They'll only give you a New York minute, but I couldn't help but wonder, isn't that enough?

Maybe for her. It's an attractive argument, but as I keep telling you, I am not she. I'm not ready to choose. So thank goodness for all these audacious Southern weddings that keep me coming back. Every summer, the invitations pour in, and every time I respond, s'il vous plait, "yes." When one ends, another begins, on constant repeat in my life. They'll always be there; they'll never change. I'll always go.

And yes, this back-and-forth behavior is taxing: monetarily, mentally, emotionally. But I am up for the challenge. I'm a brick house.

High-Fiving in

Paradise

The first thing I noticed when we pulled into the driveway was a plump jack-o'-lantern with a "W" carving instead of a face. It was Sunday, October 31, 2004, two days before the presidential election, and I was in Jacksonville, Florida. The purpose of my trip was twofold: to volunteer for an organization called Election Protection, which aims to secure the voting process, and to visit one of my dearest friends, Sarah, who'd recently left New York for her hometown. I specifically chose Jacksonville, of the volunteer centers calling for bodies, so I could multitask this way.

But I miscalculated the reconcilability of my two objectives. Sarah's friends and family were vocal supporters of Bush. And, although Election Protection is nonpartisan, most of the volunteers, including myself, were rabidly opposed. I hadn't anticipated the divide because typically politics don't play a part in my social life. But during the 2004 election, the topic was impossible to ignore—particularly in Florida, where the wounds of 2000 were still open, particularly when the first question any of her friends asked me was, "So Jane, what brings you to town?"

The trip was schizophrenic. Case in point: Halloween. That morning, I'd whooped and hollered in support of Kerry at a rally in an African American church in one of Jacksonville's poorest neighborhoods. An hour later, I was riding in Sarah's fiancé's SUV to a picnic at her cousin's beachside house, outside of which stood guard that orange sentinel with an alphabetical scar for a head.

I have to admit, it was a clever idea. The shape of the letter even resembles a toothy grin. But to me, the carving was also unintentionally appropriate. Jack-o'-lanterns are scary, just like the Bush regime. And neither a pumpkin nor George W. knows how to speak.

This was my frame of mind when they welcomed me into their home. While I hugged her cousins and met their new infant, all I could think about was that stupid vegetable. I'd known these people since college, spent multiple spring breaks in Sarah's childhood home. Her parents have literally said I'm "family." And yet, suddenly they all had new, additional identities: "Bushies." Some of them were suspicious of me, too. It's like we were all wearing masks for the holiday. It was a very divisive time.

Early Tuesday morning, I was dispatched, in a black Election Protection T-shirt, to stand outside a poll in the same neighborhood where the rally had been. My job was to answer basic questions about casting ballots, but I wasn't allowed to offer opinions or advice. No one asked me anything, though. Essentially, my presence was meant to deter voter-fraud funny business, the perpetrators of which were assumed to be—since these voters were poor and black and therefore predicted Democrats—Republicans. Basically, I spent the morning criminalizing my opponents.

Sitting next to me was my suitcase. I'd booked my return flight for that afternoon, following this line of reasoning: "If Bush wins, I don't want to be stuck in Florida." But I had one more stop to make first. I'd called another college friend, Emily, who was also living in Jacksonville. She and I had lost touch over the years, but we've always had a way of picking up where we left off. If I could bum a ride to her home, we'd have a quick visit and then she'd take me to the airport. Deal.

Emily introduced me to her son, gave me a tour of the house, and then the three of us sat around a plastic preschool table on their porch molding Play-Doh. Within five minutes the election was on our tongues. But I wasn't concerned, even though she is a staunch conservative, because the two of us thrive on debate. We've never been much for small talk, even if it's not a dispute; we once sat up all night analyzing a Sylvia Plath poem, which I realize is a hilarious cliché. That's what our early years of college were like, before we drifted apart, or rather, before our interests did. She grew more religious; I experimented with drugs. I once heard through the grapevine that she was praying for my soul. It didn't insult me; that was just her way.

"But if Kerry does lose, won't you accept it and move on?"

"No way," I responded. "I disagree with Bush's policies. Just because he's the president, I'm supposed to go, 'Oh well, there's nothing I can do'?"

We both shrugged.

"Is part of the reason why you support him because he's Christian?" I asked.

"Of course," she said. "I don't know that it matters in a

day-to-day way, but if something horrible happens, I'd feel more comfortable knowing that the person making important decisions has Christ guiding him."

We shrugged again. There was no point in arguing. Neither of us could have changed the other's mind. Instead, we probed curiously. In New York, Christian conservatives are as rare as wildlife. I felt as if I'd come across a fawn in Central Park—one that behaved exactly the way I had read it would on the Daily Kos.

She felt comfortable enough to speak candidly, or perhaps she was just that confident in the veracity of her beliefs. All I know is that, a moment later, this came out of her mouth: "Well, you know, gays aren't born that way."

I grabbed a coloring book and a purple crayon and tried to remain calm. Surely reason would clear this up. "Why do you think that?" I asked.

"Because homosexuality is a sin. And God can't create sin."

Oh no, she *was* using a reason—based on a different set of rules, yes—but logic nonetheless. "But that would mean it's a choice, and how can you explain why someone would choose to live a more difficult life?" I pressed.

"I think they turn that way because they were molested."

"On what basis?"

"My hairdresser told me."

Although it had only been a few years since Emily and I had seen each other, our two worlds had evolved to the point of having different sets of governing physical laws. I wondered, sitting on that sun porch, If I throw a ball, might it fall up?

I stole a glance at her son. Either he wasn't listening or he'd heard it all before. Sunlight streamed through the windows. My knees jutted awkwardly from the playschool chair. We all had colored clay under our nails.

So ended our bipartisan experiment. Conversation remained innocuous for the rest of my visit, full of long pauses and awkward shifts in tone and pitch. Something had changed and we both knew it.

Soon it was time to leave. She offered me a can of soda for the road, and when I popped the steel tab, a single drop of fizz arched through the air and landed on the kitchen tile. I turned to the roll of paper towels by the sink and tore a small corner from the next sheet.

"I do that too!" she exclaimed. "Why waste an entire piece on a tiny spill?"

"It's ridiculous," I agreed eagerly. "Use only what you need, right?"

We were beaming.

"Exactly. My husband is always making fun of me. He's like, 'Just use the whole thing.' And I say, 'The perforations on a roll of Bounty are merely a suggestion.'"

No one gets this excited about paper products.

When I landed at LaGuardia Airport that evening, a voice mail from Emily had traveled with me. She told me she'd enjoyed seeing me and said she was happy we felt the same way about conservation, that in spite of our disagreements, we could still find some common ground on which to stand.

I sat in my window seat, knees once more jutting awkwardly, and cried—because I was touched by her effort to bridge the divide, because I was deeply saddened by the comments causing that divide, and, mostly, because I was afraid. What we'd found was a very small patch of common ground, indeed.

If I move home, won't such small plots of land sit constantly in the shadows of towering differences? While I'm in New York, my life is a mystery to my friends in the South. If they don't see me sitting in their church in Raleigh on Sunday morning, they don't assume I'm damned—they don't assume anything at all.

As long as I am five hundred miles away, it is impossible to measure the distance between us. Our friendships exist in a kind of suspended animation. They reside within the benefit of the doubt.

At home, I would either be a member of a congregation or not, in an exclusive club or not, at a political fund-raiser or not. Inaction is still an action. Not so in New York, where I don't have to be one thing or the other. Living in purgatory is not about being free to make whatever choice you want; the city offers something more profound, a third option: immunity from making choices at all, and therefore from the judgments accompanying them. Purgatory *is* Paradise.

But now that I know, doesn't that mean I'll be expelled? Sitting on Emily's porch, I felt shame. It was cowardly of me not to stand up for my gay friends. And it is cowardly to live a life without making choices.

But I don't want to fight—not with strangers on the streets of New York, not with the people I love back home, not with anyone. I just want to high-five. I only want to high-five. If I ever leave Brooklyn, though, there might be spills. And they'll probably be bigger than a drop. So God grant me a roll of Bounty.

The gypsy
in Me

What if I showed you a still image? In it we see: my parents, me, a fir tree gilded with ornaments and lights, and a box wrapped in ribbons that bears a card reading "For Jane, Love Mom and Dad." A priori knowledge enables you to reason that an evergreen decorated as such is a Christmas tree, that gifts are exchanged on Christmas Day, that a ribboned box is a gift, that a gift's beneficiary is the person whose name appears on an attached card, and that "Mom" and "Dad" are titles for parents. Therefore one can rationally deduce that I get to have whatever is in the box. Right?

But wait; let's not be epistemologically rash. To strengthen the proof, I also present empirical, a posteriori knowledge. What if I turned that still image into a video of my mother bending down, picking up the box, handing it to me, and saying, "This is a present. It is for you, Jane, because today is Christmas, which is why we have that tree!"

Now would you believe I get the box? Plato, Aristotle, and Kant would. But you'd all be wrong (at least you were in good company), because, in this case, that which is, in fact, is not.

For if there actually were a video of this situation, here is what you'd witness directly after I opened the box.

"Mom!" I exclaim. "It's beautiful. Thank you!" I pull from the tissue paper a Herend china dish, a large upturned leaf painted forest green with delicate white veins. It is indeed a beauty.

"I'm *so* glad," she replies. Then she pauses, allowing me a few precious seconds with the item before singsongingly adding, "OK, darlin': Now wrap it up and hand it back."

Then you would see me sigh in resignation and do as I am told, so accustomed am I to the pattern of receiving gifts I cannot keep. It happens most frequently on Christmas mornings or major birthdays, whenever the gift is of a certain class: shiny things, things that shatter, hand-painted objects, stuff that requires polishing, items older than I am...if you and I were playing *The $25,000 Pyramid* with Dick Clark, and you shouted, "Lady things!" we'd hear *Ding! Ding! Ding!* and then pump the air with our fists.

I'm occasionally given such presents; I never get them. It's like a waiter bringing your dinner, letting you smell it, and then taking it away. It's like wasting fifteen minutes hitting on one of those married men who don't wear rings. I *hate* that.

Mind you, my mother won't return the Herend leaf or give it to someone else. She will put it in her basement, with all the others, where it will wait for me until a date TBD when it is TBEnjoyed. Simultaneously, they are gifts and not gifts, mine and somehow not mine. The rules governing the universe do not apply in my parents' home; I guess when my dad used to say "not under my roof" he really meant it.

Now, if I wanted to, I could visit my treasures; I could spelunk through the cardboard caves and play with them the way Scrooge McDuck swims through money in his vault. But I am not allowed to take them with me, because, and now we get to the heart of the matter, such items may not travel *to New York.*

"It'll get lost up there!" my mother cries. Clearly she hasn't seen how small my apartment is; the only thing I lose there is my dignity.

"It could be stolen!" she'll exclaim. Because it looks like an iPhone or a wad of cash? What does a crackhead want with china?

"You'll break it!" she charges. OK, Mom, you got me there: An item is more likely to shatter if being used than if cocooned in bubble wrap nowhere land.

Whatever the reason, she didn't want this particular china leaf to fall too far from the tree.

Listen, I realize how lucky I am to even kind of sort of get such unique, pricey, occasionally priceless items. This is exactly why I want them! What's the point of owning something if you can't enjoy it? How can something have a use if it can't be used? While the box is closed, it is impossible to determine whether or not the object inside is beautiful, just as it would be impossible to determine whether or not a cat had died from radiation-triggered poison. My mother has unwittingly proved the theorem of Schrödinger's silver goblet.

And if she's in the business of challenging quantum mechanics, then she certainly won't be swayed by my flimsy pleas.

"I'm surprised you wouldn't *rather* leave it here?" she kindly replies. "Then you won't have to worry about it. Just let me keep it for you." Keep it till when?

Aha: exactly.

The unspoken purpose of retaining these items is that they will be ready for me when I *come home*. Crystal vases and Herend figurines are grown-up items; they belong in the houses of people who've settled down. This line of thought betrays two assumptions: one, that I am not yet an adult, and two, that when I become one, it will not be in New York.

The first assumption is uncontested: I wake up at noon. I say things like "duh-ee" and "der." I tape fortune-cookie fortunes to my mirror and honestly gain inspiration from them. As for the second assumption...I don't know. I can't predict. My mother, however, appears to be certain: Brooklyn is a phase. My real life, the one adorned with my grandmother's pearls, is waiting for me in North Carolina. She doesn't say so; she would never pressure me. But her actions betray her. She's hoarding loot!

And anyway, there is a precedent. My eldest sister, Lou, lived in New York for seven years, and then came home, got married, and filled her house with all of the beautiful things waiting: a table passed on from my father's mother that had been made out of wood paneling from her childhood home in Wilmington, a set of crystal dessert goblets that my mother's mother's best friend smuggled out of Switzerland, a silver breadbasket out of which my mom remembers her granny serving rolls every single Sunday, and various other antique centerpieces, lamps, and pieces of jewelry, all of which have a history and are delivered with origin stories tied to their wrists.

And Tucker, my middle sister, who'd moved to New York a few years prior after getting her MBA, had just announced that she and her boyfriend were making plans to come back to Raleigh, engagement imminent. After receiving the news, Aunt Jane called me and actually said, "Two down, one to go." Tucker and her husband now sleep in the bed in which my grandfather was born.

It's the reverse of the prodigal son; they parade before me the fatted calves, telegraphing that if I find my way home, there will be one hell of a feast. "But what if I stay in New York after I get married?" I ask. "Or what if I never marry? What if I always have roommates?"

"We'll cross that bridge when we come to it" is all my mother replies. The box in the basement may as well be labeled "Dowry: to be paid at the marriage of Jane to Dixie Land." It's an incredibly patient bribe.

Or maybe I'm inferring something unimplied. Perhaps there is no subtle ruse. My mother might honestly believe there are "Borrowers" in Brooklyn who take things while you sleep. She may sincerely fear a tear in the matrix, through which tea-and-creamer sets are pinpointed and vacuumed. And who knows? She could be right; I mean, the woman *is* bending time and space in her basement.

Either way, one thing is certain: these items are currently being protected from the North. Southern families have a long tradition of doing so.

Toward the end of the Civil War, on his march back north, after the devastation of Atlanta, one of Sherman's generals, John Schofield, commandeered my father's grandfather's house in Goldsboro and turned it into his headquarters. My great-grandfather (yes, there's only one "great" there; the men in my family procreate late) was six when he watched the Yankees march down Chestnut Street and up to his front door. His mother had already buried the jewelry and silver—which are still in the family—but a horse is harder to hide. The soldiers stole my great-grandfather's pet Shetland pony. Schofield wasn't one of the "scorched earth" generals, though, so he made his men return the pony. But then they stole it again... returned it again... and stole it a third and final time when they marched out of the Carolinas for good.

Curiously, they left something else behind, an anonymous silver samovar, bearing the monogram of some other family who hadn't been quick enough with the shovel. With no way to find its owner, my great-great-grandmother kept the piece. Later, it moved with my great-grandfather into the house down the street, where my father would eventually fall under its spell. He remembers studying the monogram, inspecting the samovar for clues. But he doesn't remember the letters or, unfortunately, the cousin to whom it was willed; once again, the heirloom is lost.

Of course, my mother isn't specifically, intentionally hiding things from the North. Nonetheless that is precisely what's happening. And so, for me, moving to New York was like crossing over: One need carry nothing but a subway token for the river Styx. As they say, "You can't take it with you."

In my mother's defense, if I were allowed to bring that green-leaf dish with me to Brooklyn, I very well might break it. But the suspicion that I'd misplace it is shortsighted. How could I when it would stick out egregiously?

"What did you say was 'pretty'? Oh, that—the one thing that's not from the Salvation Army? The thing between the stack of graphic novels and the skateboard? Not the oversized plastic light-up candle that my roommate pulled in off the street after Christmas, and not the glitter snow globe I made out of an empty salsa jar, but the thing that is in fact 'pretty'? Thanks. My mother gave it to me."

But I can't make this argument to her, because it would actually hurt my case. If Mom saw where I was living in Williamsburg, Brooklyn, she would not only keep my loot in the basement, but throw me in there too.

I know people in New York whose parents stay with them when they visit. When my parents are in town, they get a hotel room and I go to them. They don't see my home—ever. It's a silent understanding, a don't-ask-don't-tell policy. They want to believe I'm not living like a college student. And I want them to believe there isn't a woman in the apartment next to mine whose name is Pussy Five. Sorry to drop the p-bomb, but that's her name. And it's not my place to go changing people's names like some latter-day Adam in the Garden of Eden. I didn't even change Amanda the cat's name when I rescued her from Staten Island and Amanda is a pretty lame name for a cat—maybe not as lame as the p-bomb plus a prime number, but you see my point.

It's impossible to have my parents over. What if we ran into p-bomb-5 outside the building? "Mom and Dad, this is... [*long awkward pause*]. [*Long awkward pause*], these are my parents."

My lovely mother, wearing her cashmere cape and *Steel Magnolias* coif, would take in the hot-pink hair and combat boots, and respond—in all sincerity—"Well, hay-eee! How wonderful to meet you." My father, in his Brooks Brothers tie and tweed hat, would bow slightly and add, "We're the Bordens." Then the three of them would shake hands and explode because that's what happens when matter meets antimatter.

It's not a risk I can take. And the chances of meeting her are high; she hangs around the stoop selling marijuana cupcakes to supplement the living she makes publishing an indie zine. And even if my parents did reach my apartment without an encounter, p-bomb-5 might knock on my door to find out if the cops had come by yet to investigate the 9-1-1 call I'd made the other night regarding that gunshot down the block.

Hmm. Sounds like her name would be the least of my parents' worries.

Still, even though there is far more crime in my Brooklyn neighborhood than in Greensboro, even though crack deals transpire on my corner and my parents live next to lawyers, even though I have in fact been robbed before, my grandmother's diamond and sapphire ring would be safer in my apartment than in my childhood home, because New Yorkers do not fall prey to that silly thing called trust. I have two deadbolts on my door and bars on my window; my father doesn't lock his car because it's "an insult to the neighborhood."

It's not the neighbors he should be worried about! Even if you moved deep into the country, miles from civilization—even if you ran background checks on each in your community—you could still get *In Cold Blood*ed. Not me: I sleep soundly inside my cage. It's not so bad in the daytime, either; I don't even see the bars anymore. Many Southerners believe that under constant suspicion is no way to live, but I find comfort in the peace of mind it engenders. It's like living in a cell. And prisoners don't get shivved in their cells.

Violent burglaries are rare in my parents' neighborhood, as is breaking and entering in general, but the area still suffers a high incidence of theft due to the kind of robbery that happens in broad daylight through unlocked doors. Every fall and spring, like clockwork, while homeowners tend gardens or walk dogs, their sideboards are unburdened by the gypsies.

Now—wait—whoa—I don't mean gypsies as in Gypsies, as in the Romany people, who've been persecuted for centuries. I'm talking about a group of petty thieves who are *referred to* as gypsies. Possibly they are indeed of Romany descent, are the dreaded example that makes discrimination against their race so hard to overcome. Or maybe, because they're foreign and they steal, Southerners just call them gypsies.

But trust me, if my liberal mother thought her words could be construed as bigoted, she'd be appalled. And you can be sure she doesn't know because she called them gypsies to their faces. Or at least she intended to. Once, before a long vacation, she hid my grandmother's silver service in the basement and left this note on the door: "To the gypsies: Our silver has already been stolen." In retrospect, actually, there is no way they read that note because had they, we definitely would have been robbed.

Look, I'm not trying to make excuses. I don't mean to justify the use of slurs. I'm reluctant to associate this band of thieves with the Romanies not least because it inclines my bleeding heart to just give them our silver as some small reparation. But the bottom line is, I don't know who they are, and furthermore neither does it matter: This story is not concerned with them but with the way they are perceived.

The gypsies are really good at what they do. They'd have to be to dupe their targets year after year, using the same techniques and on the same appointed dates. You'd think we'd see it coming, but Southerners cherish their genteel trust the way girls keep stuffed animals beyond grade school.

Here's how they work. The thieves never enter a locked door, presumably because of legal ramifications. From a distance they watch a homeowner's movements, waiting for him or her to be indisposed: in the attic, in the basement, in the shower. Then, swiftly, a woman and a man—they almost always work in coed tandem— walk nonchalantly through the front door. The woman plays decoy while the man locates a makeshift sack. If at any point she is discovered, she will become distressed, crying either about a lost dog— "Have you seen it?"—or that she feels faint—"Could I have a glass of water?"

Meanwhile, her partner fills his sack. Whatever jewelry can be found quickly is snatched. But he's on a tight time schedule and does not bother himself with what is hidden, especially not when the real prize is always in plain sight.

Almost every house in Irving Park, where I grew up, has a silver service; no society Southern home is complete without one. There are seven deadly sins, seven seals of the Apocalypse, seven veils in Salome's dance, and seven pieces in a proper silver service: coffeepot; teapot; an urn; three bowls for cream, sugar, and waste; and the tray.

This is what the gypsies want. The focus of their organized crime, their business, is singular. Or at least it is in my parents' neighborhood. Perhaps after leaving Greensboro, they hit Tennessee for gold-plated statues of Elvis.

The escape is tactical. If the loot is conspicuous or the way not clear, they will assess expedients in the landscape. A monogrammed L.L. Bean tote bag filled with sterling might be stashed in a neatly hedged English boxwood or a prodigiously flowering azalea. Later under the cover of night, another in the gang will retrieve the booty, which the grieving previous owners never knew was still under their noses. Typically though, the intruder, brazen as he clearly is, will walk directly out of the front door, carrying a suitcase, and head down Country Club Road or up Sunset Drive, like a bad Santa, until the getaway car concludes its residential-block orbit. This is when poor Gene Willoughby exclaimed, while turning into his driveway, "Huh! That man has the same luggage I do!"

Oh, Southerners are so trusting…until suddenly they are not. For it was only moments later that Gene Willoughby got wise and sounded the alarm. A network of cordless phones spread the warning call through the neighborhood.

"The gypsies are back; they got the Willoughbys."

"No! The silver?"

"Yes, the silver."

From there, information is disseminated to all family members. "Lock the door, all the time, even when we're home." Apparently the end of the directions includes, "then forget I said this and feel safe again, at which point stop locking the door for another six months, on the dot, until someone else gets robbed and we have this conversation again."

Even after the word is out, the gypsies are able to hit a few more houses before leaving town. It's as if they know who will talk to whom, who is friends with whom; as if they watch us, know who plays bridge together and who chaperones which Girl Scout troops.

Or maybe they're simply reckless—to wit, they were once caught. It was in the early '80s, and my friend Andrew's father, Locke Clifford, a prominent criminal defense lawyer, was assigned to represent one of the accused as part of his pro bono work. I called him up recently to jog my memory.

"So you want to know about the flying saucers, right?" he asked.

"The what?" I responded, wondering exactly how foreign Greensboro thought these people were.

"You want to know about the *jeepsies*!" he clarified in an accent that instantly made me homesick.

"Oh, yes sir," I said. "I do."

"It starts with the flying saucers."

Here's what happened. Someone among the recently robbed actually caught a glimpse of the getaway car and called in the description, which went out on an APB. Within a couple of hours, the police pulled over two vans. Unable to fit all of the suspects in the patrol car—and one supposes, unwilling to wait for backup—the cops decided to follow the vans to the station. At an intersection along the way, however, the two vans split in opposite directions at top speeds, forcing the patrol car to choose one and lose the other. Then, the passengers in the pursued vehicle, in an effort either to dump the contraband or discombobulate the fuzz, started throwing silver from the windows and doors. Shiny, glimmering trays and bowls Frisbeed through the air.

"The cops said it looked like something out of *Star Wars*," Mr. Clifford recalled.

Eight suspects were caught and set to be tried in federal court, as they were accused of similar crimes in towns all over the South. Each received a different court-appointed lawyer. In the middle of jury selection, however, a twist:

"Down the aisle walks this young lawyer," Mr. Clifford told me. "Black hair, dark skin, who'd been sent down from up north by the king of the Gypsies."

"Hold on," I interjected. "Did they use the phrase *king of the Gypsies?*"

"Well now, I don't remember; it's possible we assumed that. The implication was that this person was the boss. I asked, 'Are you gonna represent all eight?' The answer was yes.

"They were all sitting in the front row in the courtroom, with their arms crossed. And then they all started yakking away in a different language, and slowly the accused started leaning forward and then nodding. A few minutes later, the lawyer turned around and said, 'All right, Judge, we are ready to proceed and they've all changed their pleas to guilty.'

"Each got about three years' prison time. I was stunned. I'd never seen anything like it."

For a city like Greensboro, this was high drama. The story fueled the Harris Teeter produce-aisle gossip circuit for weeks. People couldn't believe they'd actually been caught and sentenced!

As a teenager, I desperately wanted to run into one. I wanted to stare into the face of a gypsy and see who stared back. I wasn't afraid because I knew they weren't violent. I just wanted to *meet* one and, I don't know, get his autograph? Although they meant us harm, we were strangely attracted to them. Like the way teenage girls are obsessed with vampires. Except, actually, vampires can't come inside unless you invite them. So I guess, the best comparison my childhood mind could make is that gypsies were kind of like zombies—dangerous, sure, but all you had to do to stop them was lock the door.

My aunt Jane encountered one, or thinks she did, years ago while tending to her roses in Raleigh. When she stepped into the garage for a trowel, she heard the front door open upstairs, and then footsteps directly above her. She walked to the staircase and called my uncle's name but he did not answer. Now I will hand her the microphone: "So I grabbed a coat hanger and straightened it out. And I screamed up the stairs 'I'm coming to get you! I know you're a gypsy and I'm coming to get you—you better run!' But by the time I got upstairs whoever it was was gone."

I half expect her, at the end, to pull out a flashlight, place it under her chin, turn it on, and say, "Sometimes at night, I can still hear them rifling through my underwear drawer."

Like I said, high drama. I recently asked my mom what she remembered about the arrest from the early '80s, and like any good bit of gossip, the details had been warbled during their journey through the telephone: "The king of the Gypsies himself strolled into the courtroom—dressed beautifully, in a very elegant suit—and said he'd come from New York to get them off."

"Are you sure?" I asked.

"They said he was very glamorous. He's probably dining at Jean Georges in Manhattan tonight."

For the next few days, she left me intermittent voice mails saying, "Jane, you better not write about the gypsies! They'll come get you! The king lives in New York, Jane. He's gonna get you!" Then, I'd hear her howling with laughter before the phone hit the receiver. For you to get the joke, though, you'll need more context. Really, she was making fun of her own mother, Nana.

When Mom grew up in the late '40s and early '50s in Danville, Virginia, a small town near the North Carolina border, an itinerant community came through every spring in caravans, out of which they sold tonics and told fortunes. They were known to locals as Gypsies. It's safe to assume these nomads were in fact Romanies, whose presence in that area at that time—and in that way—has been well documented.

In Danville, they squatted on a couple of acres at the end of Broad Street, which belonged to Mr. Dibrell, who owned the Dibrell Brothers Tobacco Company; he didn't mind. From what my mother can remember, the women wore multiple bracelets, head kerchiefs, long flowing skirts, and jangly earrings. "No one had pierced ears back then," she says. "If you had pierced ears, you were a gypsy." If this is true, then the Piercing Pagoda at the mall stole its imagery from the wrong culture.

Eventually, whether or not they were guilty, the nomads developed a *reputation* for stealing—another occurrence common to the time. The police began to monitor their actions. Mr. Dibrell ran them off his land. And Nana, in an effort to deter my mother from playing with their kids, told her that Gypsies steal children and turn them into other Gypsies. In case you're skimming, I'll repeat that: My grandmother told my six-year-old mother to stay away from the Gypsies because they would "steal" her.

Baby theft was a common accusation against the Gypsies—as the slander went, kidnapping was a recruiting tactic—but I don't say that to cut Nana slack. She wasn't above using scare tactics to exert influence. When she asked me, at the age of six, what I wanted to be when I grew up, I answered, "a cheerleader." For whatever reason, she found this reply unsatisfactory, so she responded, "No, no honey: Cheerleaders get diseases."

This terrified me. I remember watching football games with

my dad and thinking, *Oh, those poor girls; I hope they don't die,* and also, *Why would anyone choose that profession?*

Similarly was my six-year-old mother terrified of the Gypsies. She has a vivid memory of encountering one woman in particular, who was walking with her barefoot child toward Main Street. My mother stopped in her tracks, turned white, flipped on her heels, and fled in abject terror for home. And who can blame her? I would've done the same thing at that age if I'd been approached by a man in a van offering candy—which is essentially how my grandmother had framed the situation.

"You *ran* from her?" I asked.

"Yes! It's horrible," she replied. "Nana told me they'd take me! What could I do?" Then she laughed over the absurdity of it all and said, "Oh well."

I'll tell you this much, though. She's never pierced her ears.

The day after Christmas, the one on which the green Herend leaf dish was received and instantly retrieved, my mother insisted that my sisters and I "go through those boxes in the basement and divvy it all up."

I was confused. Was I being forced to share my future loot? I mean I guess it's only fair. Otherwise it would be like when parents turn a dead child's bedroom into a mausoleum—at least let my sisters play with my toys.

But I was wrong. These were different boxes entirely. They were the mother lode of all buried Southern treasure TBE at a point TBD, and I hadn't known they existed. I knew, of course, that both of my grandmothers had died, but because I was living in New York, I hadn't witnessed the distribution of their valuables. The boxes to which my mother referred held my sisters' and my allocations, the paltry consolation prizes you receive when you trade one box in the ground for another.

We descended the dusty catacomb stairs with a card table and chairs and took inventory: gold-rimmed crystal goblets, silver liqueur glasses, a set of Wedgwood, white and gold Nippon, green-rimmed china, a pink-and-white breakfast set, several different collections of demitasse.

We didn't recognize most of the items. In one case, there was a clear explanation. The date on the *Richmond Times Dispatch* wrapped around a set of C. H. Field Haviland Limoges china read Tuesday, December 10, 1957. Nana must have packed the plates before they moved from Broad Street to Hawthorne Drive in 1958. But she never unpacked them, not even when she moved again to Greensboro after my grandfather died. For the last fifty years, that china has lived in three basements—and counting—without being used.

In one sense, that makes it more valuable. The Haviland was one of the few complete sets in the inventory. At the same time, however, it carries no memories; its teacups are empty. *Use* is not a dirty word. Another of her sets, for example, is missing salad plates. Therefore, even if I don't remember ever eating off them, I can at least close my eyes and imagine her dropping one on the kitchen floor.

For this reason, I became more interested in the newspaper around the Haviland than in the plates themselves. I tried to conjure her wrapping them—right around the time that 6 CANADIAN SHIPS CATCH 636 WHALES, as reported by the *New York Times*, Sunday, October 20, 1957; "Virtually every part of the whale has a commercial use." While she sacramentally mummified those saucers, ALBERT

CAMUS WINS NOBEL PRIZE IN LITERATURE, Sputnik "beep-beeped triumphantly in outer space," and, my favorite, BRITAIN PRESSES U.S. ON AGREEMENT TO DUMP OIL WASTE ONLY FAR AT SEA.

It's possible that Nana intended to use her Haviland again, but simply forgot it. Or perhaps she imagined this day, when someone would roll away the stone to reclaim the contents of the tomb. Instead, time after time we only check on the body and roll the stone right back. My back ached. My nostrils were full of dust. I'm sick of these burials. Raise them up! Resurrect the dead!

But my mother is right: I couldn't schlep a case of crystal to New York unscathed. And even if I did, I've nowhere to put it. Lou and Tucker have glass cabinets for storing, and dining room tables for entertaining. My mother keeps five sets of china in the kitchen—and she uses them all.

Which means that fifty years from now, when I see the butterflies on her Queen Victoria or the Meissen's delicate orange flowers, I'll remember how she made us wear hats on Christmas Eve. I'll think about the way she'd always join a dinner party while still wearing her red-peppers apron. How she'd fill a bowl with ice cream, put it on a saucer with a silver spoon, eat it in bed, go back downstairs to refill it, eat the second serving in bed, go back down, and so on.

What if, when my children find my boxes in a cellar, they think of only the newspaper headlines? Actually, we won't even have that in common; they'll be more interested in the fact that news was once printed on paper.

My nephew Franklin appeared at the top of the basement stairwell. He was in that "Why?" phase, asking questions that inexorably lead to other, harder-to-answer questions. And I was in that smart-ass stage, because I've never outgrown it, so I couldn't help but egg him on.

"Can I come downstairs?" he asked.

"No," Lou replied.

"Why?"

"There's nothing down here for you," she said.

"Not for another forty years," I added.

"Why?" he asked. "What is that stuff?"

"These aren't toys, sweetie," she responded.

"Well," I said, "technically they are."

"Then why aren't you playing with them?" he asked.

I looked at Lou, but neither of us had an answer.

That night, while everyone else was asleep, I crept down to the living room and swiped that Herend green-leaf dish. It was still sitting in its wrapping paper by the Christmas tree and I stole it. I put it in my suitcase, and the next day, when the coast was clear, I walked it directly out of the house, into the car, out to the airport, and into my Brooklyn apartment, where it sits now on a chest of drawers.

I use the crap out of it. I put my iPod in it, my passport. Stamps, lip glosses, an old watch, Post-it notes, receipts, anything really, including items far beneath its grooming and heritage. But I think it's happy. It's hard to know for sure, it being a dish and all. But I'm pretty sure it is.

What I wish I had, though, is that samovar. It can't find its way home either, but I guarantee, wherever it is, it's shiny.

Show Us
Your Mitts

I can't fall asleep at night unless something momentous happened during the day. Obvious examples include promotions, major cultural events, and so on, but tiny triumphs also suffice. Bumping into Debbie Harry on her way out of a West Village head shop, trying a new flavor of Doritos, and high-fiving a fellow skateboarder coasting by have all, in the past, been enough. But in New York, the city of happenings, moments compete for consequence, constantly one-up each other.

Increasingly, I find that typically important events feel unworthy. I've moved beyond the pleasures of corn chips—even those cool ones with two flavors in one bag, which, let's all admit, are pretty rad. As night falls, I grow fearful of lying awake, lamenting a wasted day. So instead I go out in search of something to throw the hours at.

That is how I wound up watching two men wrestle at 5:30 a.m. in a dominatrix's apartment under the Williamsburg Bridge.

And still thought, *Ho-hum*.

It was a "Once in a Lifetime" moment. You know the Talking Heads lyrics: *"And you may find yourself in a beautiful house, with a beautiful wife. And you may ask yourself . . . Well, how did I get here?"* Except, I didn't wake up to the sterilized routines of adulthood—lawn mowing, carpooling, PTA—wondering what happened to my punk-rock youth; I did the reverse. I opened my bloodshot eyes to see a grungy unfurnished apartment, an elevated J train rumbling outside, and a plastic cup of warm vodka in my hand. Wasn't I supposed to be living in Raleigh, married to a banker, and driving a Volvo wagon? Instead of a handsome husband, I stood next to a hipster dominatrix in cutoff jean shorts. "And you may tell yourself, This is not my ironic T-shirt! And you may tell yourself, This is not my vinyl collection of the Velvet Underground! And you may ask yourself, my God—when did 'jorts' become stylish?!"

I was only supposed to be in New York one year. Two, max. But somehow I jumped the curve. And now I'm lost in the woods. I'm a ghost in the machine. *I'm not supposed to be here.*

Oh, but I love to visit, of course! And I do pretty often. A couple of times a year I come to the fashion markets in Manhattan to buy clothes for the darling boutique I opened in Raleigh with one of my old sorority sisters. And every few years, my husband flies us up to catch a Broadway show. And, then, of course, every now and then, when I need a quick escape from my marriage and mortgage, I spend a weekend partying with my crazy friend Jane who's still in New York even though she's single, broke, and lives with strangers. I mean, have you even *heard* of Craigslist? Apparently anyone can go online and—

Oh, wait . . . I got confused . . . sorry. Who am I in this hypothetical scenario? Where am I? It's dark in the woods.

The night I wound up under the Williamsburg Bridge began, innocently enough, by barhopping. My friend John, always a game enabler of trivial pursuits, met me at a dank dive called the Abbey, which I chose not only because it has a great jukebox but also because, being a Sunday, it afforded me the opportunity to tell my parents I was going to "church."

The Abbey buzzed with patrons enjoying one another's company in a convivial, straightforward manner. John and I didn't have the same goals—we like each other, sure, we enjoy hanging out, we wanted to catch up. But we were also looking for something more, literally looking over each other's shoulders during the "how was your week?"s to ensure we wouldn't miss anything of interest. Maybe someone's dog would start doing backflips, or Arcade Fire would walk through the door. Maybe the bartender would spontaneously combust. There was no way of predicting. That's the thing about New York moments: You can't make them happen, you can only catch them when they do.

One night, while walking on South Fifth Street with my friend Kurt, this surfer-looking guy with blond dreadlocks jumped out from between a bush and a trash can in someone's stoop-side front lawn, and said, "What's up? I'm Joel!"

Kurt and I looked at each other, as if to say, "Do you see the leprechaun stoner too?" I mean, he leapt, he literally leapt from behind a trash can, like a friendly Oscar the Grouch. There was still a wrought-iron fence between us when Kurt asked, "Dude, what are you doing in someone's garden?" Joel was from Seattle; he had lost his friends. He was all gangly and boisterous, like a hippie golden retriever, and he wanted to hang out. So Kurt and I said, yes, we would hang out. We bought him a drink on Grand Street, and then sent him back into the bubbling New York ooze from which he'd sprung.

That is why John and I had to split our attention at the Abbey, because you never know when you'll be visited by a leprechaun, and they are the only ones who can lead you to the buckets of gold. But everyone at the Abbey was what we weren't: happy just to be with each other. Self-actualization rarely breeds excitement. So we threw back our round and left.

"Black Betty?" John asked.

"Sure," I said.

Sunday was Brazilian night at Black Betty. But, just to be clear, there would be no Brazilians there. On Sundays, the DJ played samba music. Although, actually, there would be no samba dancing. The floor more closely resembled a trampled anthill: Dancers moved without direction and, somehow, in all directions at once. It was the sort of happening hot mess Peter Sellers might accidentally stumble into and mumble, "Oh goodness, pardon me, ouch!" before becoming tangled in someone's bell-bottom, falling over, and exclaiming, "But if that's not *my* hand, whose is it?!"

It was as if the crowd had only ever heard about samba from someone who'd watched a documentary about it directed by Margaret Mead. But they weren't distracted by their shortcomings, weren't self-conscious. They were in tune with the present, in sync with each other—needing nothing more than the beat and the calories in their bloodstream to push through each moment and into the next in a stream of energetic expression that beckoned us to join, to let go.

Borrrrring.

John and I locked eyes, nodded in agreement, and left.

I'm aware that this is disgusting behavior. I wish I could want the life my friends and family have back home, grilling lean chicken, listening to lite FM, painting nurseries, kissing their husbands, *and going to sleep.* Instead I shambled aimlessly through the streets of Brooklyn like a zombie searching for food, something I was unlikely to find as anyone with brains was already in bed.

About this insomnia thing…I know what you're thinking: a restless New Yorker? How unsurprising. Believe me, I know: New York is the city that never sleeps and neither do its inhabitants. No wonder we have a reputation for being unfriendly! You'd be too on four hours a night. We can't sleep because we're overstimulated. At least I admit it. Most New Yorkers refuse to attribute the problem to the city itself, relying instead on a number of head-in-the-sand excuses. "My job is superstressful right now." Or "I guess I've been playing too many video games." Or "I think my apartment is haunted."

They can't or won't admit that New York itself is the root of their problems. "Can't" because no one wants to be a stereotype. Or "won't" because, and this one hurts, if New York is the problem, a solution is available: leave. For most of us, though, that's not an option. Because we're addicted.

That's the thing: It's not that I can't come down; it's that I can't get enough. Furthermore, I got hooked on New York before I even knew it was a drug. I never had the opportunity to partake recreationally because I skipped freebasing and went straight to shooting up—I moved here directly from college. If New York is the city that never sleeps, then Chapel Hill is the city that dozes often and only gets up from the couch to go to the bathroom, which is saying a lot considering some towns go in their empty beer bottles instead. Nothing against Chapel Hill; it's very hip. But it's like comparing Pluto to the sun.

And so, now I'm a junkie. I'm chasing the Dragon, or, more specifically, I'm chasing the Tranny Hooker.

During my first week in the city, I played whoopee cushion with a transvestite prostitute in the Meatpacking District. I passed him/her on my way to Tortilla Flats and s/he asked if I had a pen. I checked my bag and replied, "I'm sorry, I don't, but I have a whoopee cushion." (Must a lady explain why?) S/he replied "No way!" I said, "Yes way." Then we passed it back and forth, manufactured a few hilarious *thrbbps,* and went on our ways: I to dance to Michael Jackson in casual pumps, s/he to...do whatever it is they do.

You're thinking, "Of course you knew what they do." Generally, sure, I suppose I could have figured it out, but I'd never previously considered their existence. No transvestite prostitutes were members of the First Presbyterian Church. What I knew about modern prostitutes I learned from *Pretty Woman.* And transvestites were the good-natured hucksters in *Bosom Buddies.* I was a sheltered child.

For example, Mom didn't let me patronize water parks. Something about diseases. Therefore, when I finally met one of these neon-blue paradises at the age of thirteen, on a beach trip with a friend's family, I was overwhelmed. So amped was I for my debut run, I heeded my pal's suggestion to close my eyes while hurtling down the shadowy chute because it would be "more intense." She was right: Intense describes the feeling of breaking my nose. Intense was also the reaction of mothers scrambling to retrieve their children upon seeing my bloody face barrel out of the tunnel into the wading pool. I sat bewildered while the water slowly turned pink, while Lilliputian arms made tiny splashes and still-developing feet thrashed desperately, kicking toward the sound of mothers' high-pitched wails and away from the *Jaws* of Emerald Point. I was the reason people get diseases at water parks.

I jumped into New York with my eyes closed too. Within a week I was sharing a rubber balloon with a prostitute! Talk about picking up diseases. But the only thing I caught was a bug for out-of-the-ordinary encounters, consequence, happenings. Where does a casual thrill seeker go from there, but up? And so I wander the streets of Brooklyn like a capricious Roman seeking the Coliseum's lions-eating-Christians show, something I was unlikely to find anyhow because the locals think earnest expressions of religion are uncool.

After leaving Black Betty, John and I popped by a new bar in the building next to mine on Bedford Avenue. But we stopped short in the doorway; something was slightly off. It was too loud to be so empty. And it was a bit too, if this is possible, red. Plus, the bartender eyed us desperately. It was like the bar was *trying* to be a bar, instead of being a bar. And it was trying too hard.

John and I needed a drink, not a mirror into our souls.

I remembered I had two airplane bottles of tequila in my messenger bag—seriously, must a lady explain why?—and suggested we shake our losing pattern by christening a drinking hole of our own. On some parts of the East River shoreline, if you climb over industrial fencing or squeeze through gaps in it, you can perch on forgotten rock beds at the water's edge and watch the show that is Manhattan.

I frequently wind up in one of these spots. As you've no doubt noticed, I am a wanderer, and the river is where the sidewalk ends. There have been times when, after flossing and brushing and putting on my pajamas, I find myself, forty-five minutes later, back in street clothes and sitting on the rocks. I come for the sound track. If New York City is a testament to the human imposition of order on chaos—a flattened landscape bearing grids of streets dotted with rectangular buildings populated by rows of potato chips and candy bars and filled with the dulcet A, A, B, A, B, B drones of Beyoncé— then the sound of innumerable, indistinct waves slapping against a random configuration of rude shapes, without a beginning or end to its pursuit, is one of the brain's few respites from the forced labor of perpetual pattern recognition. Without a map, the mind is released. Conscious thought slowly erodes into dreams; being awake slowly dissolves into . . .

"Pass the booze," John said. We sipped tiny bottles, like delicate alcoholics. John told me about growing up in Manhattan. By the age of twelve, he'd "seen it all." First, he became a skinhead. Then, he became a lawyer. Now he's a writer or, as I like to put it, somewhere in between.

If you mapped this tendency, it would look like a heartbeat on an ECG machine. It starts out straight. But we get bored, we want more. So we run far and fast, spiking dramatically. So far and fast that our internal bungee cord snaps us back, careening past home base on a new route down. That's not right either, though. So we wind up back where we started. Then we forget how it all happened and do it again. And again. And again.

So, sure, there's no point in running and there's no point in fighting. But we will anyway. It's just what we do. Heartbeats keep us alive.

Manhattan was gorgeous. And since John and I were alone on the rocks, when she winked, we knew it was at us. "It's almost last call," he said. "One more round?" I was tired. I was bored. I wanted to go home. I said, "Yes."

We hit the first bar we found: empty. "This is the end of the road for me," I said. John and I clinked our glasses, sighed. Just then the door swung open. A bevy of revelers paraded in and fell upon us.

"I think the Asian girl is a dominatrix," John said.

"Why?" I asked.

"Because she told me." The madam in question looked five-feet-zero and hardly old enough to drink, much less spank. Then again, maybe this was how she paid her way through college, like Tori Spelling in the Lifetime movie *Co-ed Call Girl.*

I glanced at the two boys in her harem. If she was a dominatrix, they'd been conditioned to certain behaviors, right? I swiveled on my stool, introduced myself, and, after a bit of small talk, said, "You should take your shirts off."

"Why?" one replied.

Uh-oh. I hadn't anticipated questions. "Um...because... I told you to...?" One of them shrugged. Then they both started unbuttoning. They actually did it! They took their shirts off! In a bar. Who does that? Outside of Myrtle Beach?

John shot me a scathing look and said, "Do *not* expect me to take off mine."

OK, I surmised, she was for real. That is why, when invited to her apartment for drinks, we said yes—from what I understand, you don't say no.

While we walked from the bar, in spite of the predawn chill, the two boys carried their shirts in their hands. "Are they waiting for direction?" I asked John, wondering if this was like that jinx game. If they put their shirts back on, would they owe me a Coke?

But I was too embarrassed and uncomfortable to deal with the matter anymore. Besides, I was preoccupied with our destination. I wondered how a dominatrix lives. Are there oven mitts in her kitchen? If so, are they leather? Turns out this one lived like every other twentysomething in Brooklyn, which is to say the only things of value in the apartment were an iPod and some liquor. I bet she doesn't let her parents visit either.

"Sorry," our host said, "I don't have any mixers." I poured two glasses of vodka, confirmed my suspicion that the freezer bore no ice, and handed one to John. Then I turned around to something I hadn't seen since boarding school: one guy kneeling behind another who's on his hands and knees, or, the ready position for Greco-Roman wrestling. They went at it—I mean really went at it. It wasn't erotic. It wasn't funny. It was only disturbing in the way that wrestling is *always* disturbing. They grappled and flipped each other over. Dust began to stick to their sweaty backs. Faces turned red and torsos quivered as they exhausted the last bits of energy out of each other. I'd landed at the Coliseum. I'd found my gladiators. But my thumb was unmoved to gesture up or down. Two half-naked men writhed in front of me and all I could think was, *How much does she pay for this loft?*

But this is not *my* loft. This is not my life. How did I get here? Where is my bungee cord? I've traveled too far to still feel weightless.

"I give up, John," I said. "Walk me home."

We moved in silence through the growing dawn, defeated, knowing that tomorrow's exhaustion would have no excuse, creeping along the base of the Brooklyn Queens Expressway like derelicts.

"That was strange," John said with a chuckle. Yes. But it wasn't as strange as what happened next: My mother called my cell phone.

"Hello?"

"It's a boy!" she screamed.

"What?"

"It's a boy! Lou went into labor around midnight," Mom explained. "I would have called earlier, but I didn't want to wake you."

"Don't worry about *that,*" I responded. She hung up so I could "go back to bed."

I turned to John and said, "It's a boy."

"What?"

"My sister had a baby," I said. Then I went home and slept like one.

The New York
Samaritan

You've never heard the story of the New York Samaritan?

It begins with a prophet who smelled of urine, carried his earthly belongings in a blue plastic bag, and did beseech subway riders, "Repent! The end is nigh."

A man with a briefcase approached the prophet and tried to trap him, saying snidely and with air quotes, "Master, what must I do to receive eternal life?"

The prophet parted the sea of flies to answer him, "What do the Scriptures say?"

The yuppie answered, "Love your neighbor as yourself."

"You are right," the prophet replied. "Do this and you will live."

But the man wanted to justify himself, so he asked the prophet, "Who is my neighbor?"

The prophet answered:

"There once was a man lying half dead on a path in Brooklyn; three people passed by him, including a lowly, impoverished writer named Jane.

"As the sun rose, Jane traveled the road to Brooklyn from Manhattan, where she had pimped herself as a talking head to an early-morning news program that taped in Rockefeller Center, so desperate was she for the measly media fee paid by the magazine that employed her. The man lying half dead had been working all night as well, providing relief to wicked men, peddling tiny vials filled with the unholy spirit, you know, selling heroin.

"She had passed the man, who lived in the apartment beneath hers, hours earlier while he was plying his trade. And she had said unto him, 'Sup.' But he replied not, speaking only into his phone, 'Ask and ye shall receive in exchange for twenty dollars.'

"Jane had every reason to distrust this man, for he had persecuted her. One afternoon, while she washed laundry, he picked her lock and stole the portable electronic computing device that he knew was near the front door because he'd just been upstairs to ask if the exterminator had come, and seriously there was no sign of breaking and entering so it was definitely an inside job.

"And twice she had returned home to find police vehicles flashing lights the colors of wine and sky, because he had been out turning the other cheek until his eyes did swell and his nose did break, but, man, ye should have seen the other guy.

"Alas, Jane was too poor to find new dwellings, for she had spent her last pennies, in a most desperate moment, on a Super Lotto ticket. So she remained in the haze of his hemp and Halo parties, brushing past the thieves and lepers he invited to their stoop.

"And lo, how his phone would ring through the night. And loud how the dragon chasers would shout from the street, 'Yo, Justin! I know you're there!'

"Verily, Jane had every reason to despise the neighbor, yet her heart was filled with pity, for his alcoholic, abusive parents were both locked behind the bars of the state, which is why her saint of a landlady took him in off the street in the first place. Then again, she also had gout, so neither had her path been lit by wise decisions.

"And it then happened that, while approaching India Street, on the road from 30 Rock to her bed, Jane did encounter two lums-of-the-hood fleeing the building, who spake naught to her and scurried toward the rising sun. And lo, upon ascending her stairs, she did rediscover Justin her neighbor lying half dead on the second-floor landing in the middle of her path. Where he once had conducted business, now he lay prostrate, stripped of his raiment, shaking as a man filled with evil spirits. In his pallid skin, his eyes did roll and his tongue did loll and his mouth did froth. Jane saw that he was tweaking and saw that it was bad.

"He looked to her, slowly raised his arm, grunted with great effort, and reached his hand toward her in need and in terror.

"Gazing down upon his face, Jane said only, 'Ew,' then lifted her foot, stepped over him, and continued up the stairs."

Concluded with his tale, the prophet asked the lawyer, "Which now of these three was neighbor unto him?"

The lawyer replied, "I think they're all assholes."

And the prophet said unto him, "Exactly. This is New York, you fool. Also, the aliens are trying to eat me because my hands are made of crackers. And I took your wallet."

Surface

Voodoo
Thermodynamics

*H*mm, consciousness. Yes. Now what? Something *slick and cold. Locate it, pinpoint it: face. It's resting on my face. I have a face! A cheek, in fact. Oh, I'm getting good at this. OK, but what is it, a fish? No. The tongue of a giant Arctic beast? That's ridiculous. Wait: It's not on me; I'm on it. And so are my hands. I have hands!*

I opened my eyes.

Tile. Of course: bathroom tiles. Whoa—my bathroom tiles. Yes, this is my apartment. I am a person. I'm a Jane! I live in Brooklyn. Those are my hands and that is the angle where the floor meets the wall. Check and check.

I pushed my torso away from the floor.

Blood! That is definitely blood. I know what blood is. That is it. Oh

God...hey, I know what God is too. Or, well, I know the various ways in which we perceive God. I mean no one really knows what—Focus Jane.

I tried to stand.

OK: I know those are underwear. I know those are knees. And I know that the latter is not where the former go. Aha! I was sitting on the toilet—yes, I remember now. I woke up to go to the bathroom. That is why there are sheep pajamas in a heap at my ankles. That is why it is night. It is night. That is why.

I looked in the mirror.

This explains the blood: a gash above my left eye. Actually, gravity explains the blood. This is coming together: I fell forward off the toilet and landed on my eyebrow. Man, that's rough; I'm glad I wasn't conscious for it...wait, that doesn't make any sense. Also, if that had been my trajectory, wouldn't there be correlating—yep, throbbing pain in my kneecaps.

I started to clean myself up.

Hmm, the blood on my face is dry. That can't be good. How long was I out? The puddle of blood on the floor is wet. And the gash is still moist. I could sit and time how long it takes for more to dry, or I could wipe the floor and go back to sleep.

I went back to sleep.

Medically speaking, this is what happened: micturition syncope, meaning that my brain shut down because it didn't get enough blood, due to a swift drop in blood pressure. This sudden dive was caused by vasodilation. Such an opening of the vessels occurs normally under various circumstances, such as waking from a deep sleep or emptying the bladder; the brain reacts by constricting the vessels so that blood is forced upward. However, when a body is fatigued and severely dehydrated, the vessels can dilate beyond the brain's ability to compensate. And when two otherwise normal dilations occur simultaneously—to a body already compromised—it's like delivering a one-two punch to a fighter who's leaning on the rope.

Basically, the cause was fatigue. Fatigue threw the kegger; everyone else was upstairs trying to do homework.

Figuring this out required visits to a few different doctors: one who determined I was hypoglycemic and said the problem had to do with my vagus nerve, another who guessed that I dehydrate too easily, an immunologist who ordered so much lab work that I almost fainted again during the withdrawal of thirteen vials of blood, and a gynecologist who discovered I have polycystic ovarian syndrome, which means, among other goodies, that when I'm older I'll have a mustache. Wheee!

All of these things are true, as it turns out, and each contributed to what I shortly thereafter dubbed "my Vegas experience." What medicine couldn't explain, though, or at least hasn't yet, was the aftermath. I woke up as a tabula rasa, and not only in the sense that I didn't know who or where I was; we've all had that feeling before, maybe in a hotel room or after vigorous trampoline jumping. This time was different. When I got out of bed the next morning my senses were heightened—cleared, as if something had Roto-Rootered out of me all of the gunk that clogs our receptors over time. Either that or I had superpowers.

Car horns were louder. The wind felt like needles. I smelled cigarettes on nonsmokers. I could see light breaking into crystals in mirrors. Colors were crisper and somehow more primary. And the sun, my goodness, I had to wear both shades and a visor. I tried not to go outside between ten and two.

This lasted for days, maybe two weeks. I could eat only bland foods. I was particularly sensitive to salt and sugar, the latter of which not only assaulted my tongue, but gave me an instant dizzy high. A cup of fruit-on-the-bottom yogurt made me ill. High-fructose corn syrup was like crack.

Then, slowly, I dulled again to my surroundings, returned to normal, or what I now refer to as generally accepted abnormal. But for a couple of weeks, I experienced the world as babies do, without a protective sensory filter. No wonder they love shiny objects; a wristwatch is the equivalent of a whirring, glowing UFO.

I know this sounds like hyperbole. All I have as a nonfiction writer is my word. And believe me when I say that I found it stranger while it was happening than you are finding it now. It straight up freaked me out.

I was moving through the world in slow motion, unable to ignore anything. Every tiny stimulus competed for my attention. And New York is a city of stimuli. I experienced the city unbridled; and I couldn't handle it. *Every* child born here must be a crack baby.

That cliché about becoming "numb" to something? It's backward. The image it invokes is of a wearing down, suggesting that contact with the incessant, horrific stimulus—war, animal euthanization, ice-cream-truck music—scrapes away at your nerve endings until they no longer function. But that's not how it works at all. The stimulus doesn't take a part of you with it; it leaves a part of itself behind, like the stinger of a bee. Over time, all of these little parts build up, until you're completely covered in a sweater of bee butts. They act as a shield. Et voilà: you feel nothing.

After living in New York for eight years, I was wearing one of those sweaters, and also long johns underneath, as well as a ski romper on top and, for good measure, a hazmat suit. Then, suddenly, I was naked. On the bathroom floor.

The effect was that of a rebooting, which, in addition to real pain, gave me a paranormal anxiety. The collapse mirrored too neatly my concurrent emotional state: a waxing inability to feel. It fit together a little too perfectly. I mean, come on, a psychological crisis manifests itself in a physical breakdown? A fifth-grader could have written that. It's unoriginal and trite. But I can't help that; it's just how it happened. So seriously, am I calling the shots or am I the main character in some eleven-year-old's creative-writing assignment?

My musical obsession during that time was the album *Universal Audio* by the Delgados: "See us. Watch how the city consumes us. Watch how the city destroys us." Also, right around the time I crashed, so did my computer. I can't make this up. I'd be crap if I did.

Of course, these are merely coincidences. They shouldn't mean anything. But, as Paul Auster wrote on the first page of *City of Glass*, "The question is the story itself, and whether or not it means something is not for the story to tell." That responsibility falls to the listener. Deriving meaning from fiction is a reader's most basic instinct. We even see allusions and draw conclusions where a writer didn't intend them to be.

And I posit that the fiction reader and the nonfiction writer employ the same process: We search for patterns and meaning in stories that have already been written. Therefore, instead of discounting *my* story's hackneyed climax as eerie coincidence, I am compelled to make assumptions about authorial intent. And since I don't believe in predetermination or the Fates, I am left to guess that a pockmark-faced prepubescent chubbo has created me for his final project in English class.

Well, unh-uh, sorry, out of the way, kid. If anyone will get creative with this tale, it will be me. And the first thing I'll do is throw in a dash of magical realism. If we've determined that coincidences carry as much weight as facts, then I have failed to divulge the key plot point: Around the time of my collapse, I received a cursed stone.

Did I believe that the gem was magic when I accepted it? Of course not. Do I believe now? No. Does this story give a flying flip what I do or do not believe? Not at all. The question is the story itself. And it starts in 1956.

Henry Dickerson knocked on the door of 496 Hawthorne Drive in Danville, Virginia. It was dusk. He carried a wedding dress and a small box, and he was distressed.

My grandmother opened the door. She was expecting him, as he'd called ahead to ask if he could bring a couple of things to my aunt Jane, who was sixteen at the time. His wife, Patty, had recently died.

The Dickersons were close friends of my grandparents, and my aunt was touched by the gesture. Although she declined the gown—Mrs. Dickerson had been quite petite—my aunt wanted the box. It held a five-carat, rectangular topaz, yellow-brown and clear. With my grandmother's permission, she accepted it.

They thanked Mr. Dickerson kindly, reasserted their condolences, and closed the door, at which point my grandmother announced that the stone could not stay in the house. Patty may have been tiny, but her problem with alcohol had been huge; it's what killed her. Furthermore, the Dickersons had no children. The combination of these circumstances led my grandmother to believe that her neighbors had bad luck, the kind you can catch. She then deduced—by some voodoo bastardization of the first law of thermodynamics—that the stone now carried the Dickersons' misfortune inherent, and that because they had given the stone to my aunt, the bad luck would be transferred to our own family.

Cursed or not, though, it was a nice rock. Aunt Jane didn't want to throw it out. So Nana suggested a compromise: They'd bury it in their neighbor's yard.

That afternoon, she had my aunt wrap the topaz in tissue paper and place it in a mason jar. Then, Nana rang the front bell of the Hermans' house next door. While she distracted Elise Herman with neighborhood gossip, my aunt crept behind the house, dug a hole in the side garden with a spade, put the jar in the ground, covered it with earth, and snuck back to 496 Hawthorne Drive.

There the stone remained for twenty-one years. When Elise died, long after her husband had, nearby Averette College purchased their house for its president. My grandmother, full of worry, called my aunt to come dig. Jane, now married and living in Raleigh, drove to Danville, exhumed the jar—she remembered exactly where she'd put it—and took the topaz back with her, where it sat in a chest for another twenty-eight years. Apparently my aunt Jane isn't as superstitious as her mother was. Then again, that would be difficult to achieve.

If I forgot something from Nana's house, and went back in to retrieve it, she'd make me sit down before leaving again, even if just for a second, because she believed it was bad luck to enter a home if you didn't plan to stay. The sitting down was some kind of supernatural con.

And we always walked into a house or store through the same door from which we'd left...or was it that we had to exit through the same door we entered? This one was particularly confusing for me, as I'd always lived in the same home: How could I follow a pattern if I didn't remember the way it had begun?

There were also the standbys: spilled salt, shattered mirrors. When a black cat crossed the street in front of Nana's Buick LeSabre, which happened frequently since one lived in her neighborhood, she'd slam on the brakes and put the car in park. Then we'd both get out, turn around three times, and get back in.

If you pass a truck on the street with a load of hay, don't look back at it. If you see a white horse, you must (1) make a fist with your right hand, (2) lick your right thumb, (3) swipe your wet thumb against your left palm, (4) smack your wet palm with the bottom of your right fist, and (5) repeat steps one through four twice more. Failure to execute any of these rules led to bad luck.

My first impression of superstition: kind of laborious.

But my father feared that I'd find it attractive. One night, instead of telling me stories before bedtime, he said he wanted to have a talk. I was maybe eight or nine—old enough to reason but young enough to be impressionable, not so young that I don't recall the conversation but definitely too young to remember the dialogue.

He wanted me to understand that superstition was false. It went against reason, he argued. How could returning home to grab an umbrella cause bad luck? And if it did, what would sitting momentarily on an ottoman possibly do to stop it?

Here, here, I responded. It all seemed silly to me.

More important, he added, superstition was sacrilegious. It was the equivalent of worshiping a golden calf. Unsurprisingly, he'd never made this argument to Nana, who was a devout Presbyterian and, more important, his mother-in-law, which is likely why he suggested we not tell her about our little talk. I nodded that I understood. He kissed me on the forehead and turned out the light.

Like a kid who snoops precisely where you tell her not to, I started going out of my way to walk under ladders. I still do. It is my tiny and meaningless, yet somehow satisfying revenge for every time I had to get out of that Buick and spin around. I open umbrellas inside. My soccer jersey in high school was number 13. Yes, I recognize that there is little difference between avoiding black cats and chasing them, but like I said, it *all* seemed pretty silly.

Still, silly is fun, and I was obsessed with the Tale of the Dead Alcoholic's Topaz. I simply couldn't believe they'd dug a hole in someone's garden to bury a rock—and that my grandmother had played the red herring! It was straight out of the Hardy boys. It was completely absurd.

The first and most obvious question pertaining to its burial: "If it was such bad luck, why not throw it away?" I recently interrogated my aunt.

"She figured as long as it wasn't in our home, we wouldn't get the bad luck."

"Then why not bury it in your own backyard?" I asked. "Did Nana have something against the Hermans? Was this retribution for stealing Dit?"

"Heavens no! We loved Elise and Milton. But the stone couldn't hurt them because it hadn't been *given* to them."

"But then you took it to Raleigh! Weren't you worried?"

"Well," she said with a sigh. "I figured, it was always mine. After all those years, it'd already done whatever it was going to do."

As I got older, my fascination grew. I thought about it frequently, envisioning the stone sitting in my aunt's chest, where, in my mind, it radiated light and generally stewed. Then, one Christmas morning, a few months before my Vegas experience, I no longer had to imagine. It became clear that she was giving me the topaz as soon as she started unwrapping it—regular jewelry doesn't come in a Ziploc baggie.

I was overjoyed: much cooler than a pair of socks. The rock was smaller than I'd imagined it to be; magical things typically are.

Bereft of a setting or chain, it looked lonely. Still, it felt special in my hand, strange in its lightness. Even though I knew—*I know*—that there is nothing supernatural living inside that crystal, I drew a certain power from closing it within my palm.

Later, back in Brooklyn, during a party in my apartment, the saga came up in conversation. Standing by my refrigerator and keeping an eye on a frying pan, I launched into the story, fielding furrowed-brow questions to the best of my ability.

One of my friends: "Wait." [*Eyes squint; head bows momentarily.*] "What?"

Me: "*I know!*"

A crowd began to gather. "Kate, you watch the sausage," I said. "I'll get the stone."

I scuttled downstairs, fetched the suede drawstring sack from my underwear drawer, and ran back up. The topaz was still in its plastic bag. I took it out and passed it around, like it was nothing more than silicate mineral of aluminum and fluorine. We exchanged a couple more "Wow"s and "Huh"s, and then turned our attention to my friend Brian who had pulled out a card game he'd brought called Set.

The stone must have been furious! What was it, a toy or a trophy? We were so disrespectful. I paraded it around like a monkey in diapers. But I didn't know! I didn't think it was charmed. I mean, I *don't* think it is. I don't…I don't *know* anymore. Maybe it is. Who am I to say? Here's something else my aunt told me when I interrogated her just before starting the chapter you're reading. I asked why she'd never put the gem in a setting and she said, "I only wear a few pieces of jewelry, my favorite things." Then she paused, and added, "Or maybe I was always saving it to give to you."

What?! So, all along, the stone was meant for *me*? And—oh no—she gave it to me. Gave. That means, by whatever *Gremlins*-rules logic we're following here, the focus of the gem's power was then transferred onto me, which is clearly exactly what it wanted.

What was she thinking? "After all those years, it'd already done whatever it was going to do"? All what years? Forty-eight is nothing to a rock. Those things live for millennia. It takes thousands of years just for the crystals to form. That means it was in labor for longer than Christians and Muslims have hated each other. If one dog-year equals seven human-years, then one rock-year equals...whoops, you missed it. Here comes anoth—ohp too late again.

Well, if it wanted me, it got me, coldcocked me on the loo. And just so you know, my...*curiosity*...regarding the...*potentiality*... of a hex, and my belief in the scientific definitions of human biology need not be mutually exclusive. Who's to say Snow White didn't also have low blood sugar?

Obviously, I only believe because I want to. My dad was right: Superstition is attractive. It's easy and comforting to live in a world in which the rules are already set. I know this because I'm a New Yorker.

Everything has been decided in this city. No fundamental conundrums remain. There are no paths to be cut; they're all laid out already, flattened and gilted in concrete. Life here is a cinch. Stay on the sidewalk, stop when you see an orange hand, the pigeons don't bite. That's basically it. Every New York guidebook is too long by however many pages it is minus one.

Sure, a New Yorker's life is full of tiny problem-solving opportunities. Should I pick up Thai, Indian, Ethiopian, Peruvian, Polish, or Afghani? To get home I can either take a subway, bus, cable tram, train, ferry, taxi, water taxi, bicycle taxi, or helicopter.

But those only mask the fact that all of the major decisions have already been made. What will I eat? I can either figure out how to kill that bear or invent agriculture. How will I get to my yurt, especially if I have to drag this bear?

In New York, I don't need to follow the sun to find my way—which is good considering I can't see it—because I memorized that rule about traffic flowing north on even-numbered avenues and south on the odds. How is that any different from not needing to prepare for disaster because you know how to knock on wood?

It was easier for me to believe I'd been cursed than to accept the cold, hard-bathroom-tile fact that my lifestyle was slowly destroying me. "You're burning the candle at both ends," my mother would say (thanks, Edna St. Vincent Millay).

It's just that there is so much to do and I want to do it all. If there are that many cuisines available for takeout, imagine the number of events: rock concerts, comedy benefits, book launches, TV wrap parties, art openings, restaurant openings, theater openings, even the opening of my mail is a fete if you add champagne. And of course, there is *always* an after party. You know how you can count rings in a tree trunk to determine its age? If you looked at a slice of my brain in a microscope, you'd be able to tell which weeks were spent outside of New York.

It wasn't my fault, you see. New York was tempting me. It expected me to participate, always, the way a gregarious person's friends expect her to always be "on." The city lures its inhabitants, seduces us; it's an evil hypnotist, a nefarious prankster, a . . . uh-oh, this sounds familiar. I've mistakenly followed this logic before. New York is *not* a cartoon assassin. It's not out to get me, and it doesn't care if I go to its parties. Actually, it'd probably prefer I don't; my absence could be filled by two, maybe three, models.

I mean, without doubt, the city *is* killing me. But it's because I'm running into the knife. I'm so quick to blame New York, but it's never New York's fault. Waking up on the bathroom floor felt like being thrown out of a game of Double Dutch I didn't know I was playing. I stood outside the switching ropes and perceived with incredulity how swiftly they revolved. Had I been moving that fast for that long? I find I am reluctant to hop back in.

I've slowed down. I stay home some nights. I drink water and sports drinks and have cut back substantially on sugar and alcohol. And, although half of my muscles are clenched in so doing, I sleep at least nine hours a night. I'm following the medical advice, the truth, the facts—I mean, obviously. It's not like I'd rely on a wooden knock or lack of ladders. I put no stake in superstition. That doesn't mean, however, that I've discounted the supernatural powers of the metaphor.

And so, whenever I'm riding the subway, waiting in line, or anytime I don't need to see with precision, I take off my glasses. That way, even if only for a few minutes, the whirring, glowing UFO that is New York City smudges hazily into a more manageable landscape, an impressionist version of itself. The effect is like Xanax for the senses.

Also, I still revere the topaz, but not because it's magic. I just think it's beautiful. The question is the stone itself and whether or not it means something is not for the stone to tell.

Rubber Balls for
Weapons

"Whoa," said the indie rocker as he filed through the iTunes folder on my laptop. I was making drinks; he'd been tasked with music. A pause followed his dude exclamation while, I deduce in retrospect, he continued to scroll. Then he said "Whoa" again and made that sound that resembles a cough at the start, but ends with a tiny derisive laugh, before adding, "You have a lot of James Taylor albums."

Seriously? A guest in my home was mocking my music collection? Through lips he later planned to put against mine?! This couldn't be happening. I put down the half-sliced lime.

"You don't like James Taylor?" I asked from the kitchen.

"Um, *no*," he responded as if the answer were obvious, as if I'd asked him, "You don't eat poop?"

My incredulity no longer stemmed from his brazen disregard for my hospitality. He was laughing at five-time Grammy-award-winning, Rock 'n' Roll Hall of Famer James Taylor. I was being called to crusade against ignorance. I walked into the living room.

"Are you actually familiar with his albums?" I asked, standing over him with the knife still in my hand. "Have you heard anything besides the greatest hits?"

"Well, uh, no."

"Then consider the possibility that you are wrong." I walked back into the kitchen, poured the tequila, and shot back over my shoulder, "By the way, I don't have 'a lot of James Taylor albums'; I have them all."

That was a lie. I haven't bought one since *New Moon Shine* in 1991—the lyric before "Never die young" in his 1988 hit by the same name is "Never grow old"—but I was beyond playing fair.

Don't hate on James Taylor. Just don't. My mind raced with what I wanted to say: He is the Prometheus of molasses white-boy blues; you play drums behind some guy who went to Brown. His 1970 album, *Sweet Baby James*, helped define and cement a new wave of singer-songwriters; your band sounds like three others I heard this week. James Taylor's lyrics are heartfelt and unashamed; your glasses are ironically too big for your face.

My knife split the lime with a thud.

Oh man, I was mad. It surprised even myself. As a Southerner in New York, I am accustomed to enduring slights against all manner of my homeland's characters and characteristics. Please, I was used to it before I hit puberty. In jokes on TV, film, and in cartoons, Southerners, whether real like Jesse Helms or imagined like Gomer Pyle, are frequently cast as the butt.

It doesn't faze me anymore. Call me inbred, racist, stupid, flighty, fake, Bible-thumping, backward, or red and I will not bat an eyelash. I'll probably play along: "What? God bless you, chile, but you'll have to speak up—I got the KKK in one ear and my cousin's tongue in the other." But take a crack at the man who recorded "Carolina in My Mind" and apparently my insides turn to lava.

"Awesome, you've got the Muffs," he exclaimed and clicked play on the first track of *Happy Birthday to Me*.

Typical, I thought and delivered his margarita.

After dinner we hit the neighborhood bar scene. I lived in Greenpoint at the time, a traditionally Polish area on the Brooklyn waterfront to which artists, and the hipsters who inevitably follow them, were flocking. The latter two groups acted like warring colonies in the New World; the cool and the trying-to-be-cool were engrossed in a battle for Greenpoint without recognizing the native culture's stake.

The indie rocker and I reached our destination in a few blocks. The Pencil Factory is Greenpoint's oldest and most authentic artist-hipster bar. It was packed; it usually is. The bare wooden tables and benches—the place is too cool even for decor—were full of the young and attractive. I noticed the bassist of a semifamous band sitting with friends at the far end of the bar, the teenager equivalent of the back of the bus.

We staked out a spot and I ordered a margarita.

"You don't like it?" the indie rocker asked, prompted by my pucker.

"No, it's good. It's just really tart." I got the bartender's attention and asked, "Could I trouble you to make this a little sweeter?"

I knew I'd done something wrong because the indie rocker winced. Then the bartender replied, "Uh, I could put more triple sec in it—if that's what you *want*." And then that sound again, that contemptuous laugh masquerading as cough. Do they teach you that in cool school? Besides, when did triple sec become lame? It's an orange liqueur, not a film director. It's not even a brand; it's a category. You can't stratify a liquor cabinet like *The Breakfast Club*.

"I'd love a little more triple sec," I said, smiling. Although the doctored drink was better, it couldn't eradicate the bitter taste in my mouth.

At the bottom of the glass, I told the indie rocker I had to catch an early flight. Although I did want an escape, I wasn't lying. The next morning I left LaGuardia Airport and, five hours later—via Charlotte, New Bern, and Highway 70—pulled up to the neighborhood Fourth of July block party my family was hosting in Morehead City.

It was already in full pastel-seashell-sundress effect. I meanwhile wore all black, hadn't showered, and smelled like diesel fuel. When I opened the door between the air-conditioned car and the sun-surrendered lawn, it made a sucking sound. My hair instantly curled.

The house we share with my dad's brother and sister is not on the coast proper. Morehead City lines the Bogue Sound, which is part of the Atlantic Intracoastal Waterway, a route navigable from Virginia to Florida. The Intracoastal bisects North Carolina's mainland and the Outer Banks. Across the water, we can see the city of Atlantic Beach and the ocean-seeking tourist hubbub that crowds it. Morehead is more of a community. Today they were showing their pride.

Barbecue smoke rose above the surface of an undulating sea of blond hair, and multiple mayonnaise-enhanced homemade delicacies lurked just beneath. There were about sixty people crowded around a makeshift tent on the empty lot between our house and cousin Millie's next door. Half were kin, and at least four of them went by Borden as a first name, the youngest of whom was my seven-month-old nephew, currently strapped to the chest of my cousin Nancy.

"Jane!" she screamed, like a riptide. I didn't take my bags out of the car. I didn't even go inside to wash my hands. Who knew how long the sun had already warmed those mayonnaise salads? Time was running out.

I hugged Nancy, stole my nephew, held my proverbial nose, and jumped in. My sisters were by the buffet, unsurprising as we've always congregated around food. I filled a plastic red-white-and-blue plate with slaw, ham biscuits, and a salad with bacon and broccoli in it, and then also spotted my mother by the side of the house, indulging my other nephew's fascination with the water spigot. Dad was nowhere in sight.

I took a turn on spigot duty and later revisited the tent to get homemade pimento cheese and a closer look at a neighbor's matching linen summer suit that involved lime-green culottes. No one had seen my father.

My older nephew tore across the lawn toward Millie's. Assuming that area to be out of bounds, I gave chase but, upon turning the corner, discovered a new wing to the picnic. Close to twenty more people were under Millie's porch, including my father, who lingered, I should've guessed, by the dessert table.

There were lemon squares, several kinds of pie, pound cakes, rum cakes, and iced cakes, cookies baked with various supermarket candy bars stuffed inside, brownies, blondies, a variety of treats unidentifiable, and fudge. "What's good?" I asked him.

"Well, I'm partial to the *pea*-can pie," he said in the rollicking eastern North Carolina accent that returns to him, seeping out like pine sap, whenever he's with Uncle Donnie. Donnie isn't really my uncle; he's my dad's first cousin and closest friend. In their bachelor days, they had a boat named *The After You Two*. When they double-dated, they'd tell the girls they'd "named a boat after you two."

Donnie was grilling hot dogs a few feet away. I grabbed one

because...I don't need to explain myself...hugged him and returned to the dessert quandary. "Hm, what else?" I asked with my mouth full.

"Oh tha's right, you don't like pea-cans." He pointed at something brown and said, "That one's delicious, but dadgum if I know what t'is." The treat in question was a bar of some sort; it appeared to have a graham-cracker crust, gooey filling, and, on top, glistening butterscotch chips half melted in the sun. "I'll warn you, though," he added. "It's pretty sweet."

"Good," I said. "That's how I like 'em."

I put one on a napkin, in addition to whatever I could grab quickly, as we were being called to the tent, and apparently this sort of time constraint with food causes me to act like a refugee. Once the crowd gathered and the hosts quit trying to shush the kids, an elderly gentleman I didn't know read out loud the Declaration of Independence. When he finished, everyone cheered, and then we sang "God Bless America." No one laughed; no one was being ironic.

With my treats in tow, I walked from the party toward the dock and out onto the Bogue. The wake from a powerboat impassively whapped the pilings. Barnacles blinked, licked the air, opened and closed until the water covered them again. I dangled my feet over the edge, looked out at the green and red channel markers.

Leading in to every port is a dredged path. Poles topped with green signs are staggered along the left side of the canal; reds are on the right. To avoid running aground in shallow waters outside the channel, boaters are taught a mnemonic device: Red Right Returning. Keep the red markers on the right when you're returning to your home port. Then, of course, when you're leaving port, the greens would be on the right. In the big channel, the Intracoastal Waterway, the red markers run along the mainland, so in order to apply the mnemonic device, you just need to pretend like Miami is your port. The only thing you need to remember is that if you're going south, you're going home.

Every winter, my body forgets the sun. I'm sure most of you are this way. It's rather daft of us, actually. But we'll never learn, because we're not allowed to; it's a defense mechanism. Without it, I'd spend December, January, and February pining for solar rays. Instead, I forget they exist.

It's as if, during the first frost, my brain calls a meeting with all the sun-seeking receptors in my nervous system, the loud ones who'd otherwise spend all winter poking me, "Are we there yet?" Once they're all in a room together, my brain locks the door and drones into a microphone, "You're getting *verrry* sleepy."

All winter long, while those receptors are inactive, I can only recall the sun in the abstract. I know that I like summer; I'm certain that it's nice. However, I can't place exactly why.

But, suddenly, the first sunny day of spring: *ka-pow!* It slaps every cell: Wake up! Wake up! And the receptors are all like, "Why were we sleeping in our clothes?" My whole body buzzes. I turn my face skyward and melt in the spot where I'm standing.

Then, of course, I snap out of it, throw my hand on my hip, and say to myself, "Damn, Brain: fooled me again."

This is how I forgot the South. My brain was protecting me from regional affective disorder. For nine years I lived in New York without an aching. I loved home. And I definitely missed it—but it was in the abstract. Until suddenly something changed. The long-dormant Southerner inside me stretched, yawned, opened her eyes, and said, "I wear glasses now?"

After that, she wouldn't go back down.

How else to explain why, nine years into living life as a New

Yorker from the South, I suddenly wanted to be a Southerner in New York? I started smuggling grits and relishes out of my parents' pantry whenever I went home. When I got angry, I'd say things like "dadgum-blast-it." I once called in to the NPR show *Soundcheck* because someone was bad-mouthing the banjo. And for an annual fee, I joined something called the North Carolina Society.

It's actually the oldest operating state society in New York, I soon discovered. It was founded in 1898 and is essentially a social club. I signed up just in time for the annual December dance, a swank black-tie affair held at the University Club on Fifth Avenue. Never before in New York have I had the license to ask two well-dressed people in an elevator, apropos of nothing, "Where y'all from?" Never before in this city have I bellowed from inside a bathroom stall, "I was a Tri Delt too!"

It was great fun. The pianist even played "Carolina in My Mind" during dinner. But at 10:00 p.m., it was over and I turned back into a New York pumpkin.

Fortunately, college basketball season was getting under way. There's a kid from Charlotte named Dennis Park who researches the Manhattan bars that screen Tar Heel games. Each week during the season, he e-mails his DIY list of alumni pals and announces the next location, which, for two hours, will house a sea of khaki pants and loafers. The waitstaff must think they've fallen prey to one of those flash-mob pranks: "Is something going on? Why is everyone wearing black croakies on their sunglasses?"

I picked a good year to start caring again; in 2009 we'd go on to win the NCAA Championship. The cheers and the chants were still second nature. And before long I once again knew all of the players' names and stats. Carolina basketball was back in my life, and as such, anticipation of two events in particular eclipsed my winter: our matchups with Duke University.

The rivalry is one of the oldest and most storied in all of American sports, professional or collegiate. Hatred toward Duke University—or as we call it, the University of New Jersey at Durham—runs through North Carolina as thick as pig shit in the Neuse River. My cousin Calder taught his dog this trick.

"Sugaree, would you rather go to Duke or be a dead dog?" Then Sugaree rolls over, sticks his paws in the air, and lies still.

It is the one self-evident truth we know. Pinch me: If it hurts, am I not awake? Show me a picture of Coach Mike Krzyzewski: If I wince, am I not a Southerner?

This would be my thing, my secret wardrobe passageway to home. Neither time nor distance could diminish my disdain. For truly, though winds change, flat worlds become round, space bends, and time turns dynamic, one thing in the universe remains forever constant: Duke University sucks a big one.

Basically what I'm saying is that Duke thinks those jeans make you look fat.

I really threw myself into it. When friends hosted a party for the second Carolina-Duke game, I procured a documentary about the rivalry for us to screen in advance; I tended bar during halftime. After we won, while our counterparts stormed Franklin Street in Chapel Hill, lighting bonfires and blocking traffic, my friends and I stormed the Franklin Street that runs through Greenpoint; that is, we stood on a nondescript corner intermittently leaping.

A couple of kids across the street lodged an inquiry into our humble commotion and received in return a shout involving something about a "victory." The kids ran off. We pierced the air with a few more woo-hoos and one of us tried to climb a street sign. Before long, though, our excitement atrophied to occasional clapping followed by deep sighs and a need for affirmation: "Haaah...that was fun, right?"

Then, just as we began to leave, the kids returned in legion.

They must have annexed an army at the park a few blocks away for they were now seven or eight strong and carrying water guns and rubber balls.

"Do you want to battle us now?" the ringleader asked innocently.

There is no better indication of an army's weakness than receiving a challenge from seven-year-olds whose idea of a sword is round and soft. Our real foe, meanwhile, didn't even know we existed. We were too far removed, beyond the edges of the map.

And anyway, after March Madness, Franklin Street became, once again, just another road in my neighborhood. And I went back to jonesing for home.

I didn't want to *move* home, mind you. I wanted to import it, bring it with me. The suggestion that I'd have to choose between NC and NYC seemed unfair, absurd. It's just one little Y. Why can't I have it sometimes but not all of the time like the vowels do? There had to be a way to have my cake and eat it too, and I was determined to find it.

It is in such moments of desperation that people act rashly. This is how I wound up, one April night during a particularly intense craving, crossing the kitschy threshold of Brother Jimmy's, a barbecue restaurant in New York that promises to "put some South in yo' mouth." I thought it would help, stand in for the real thing, like methadone. I was wrong.

As soon as my friend and I sat down, a pert waitress in a low-cut shirt stopped by the table and asked, "Y'all want a shot?" Then she blew a whistle that signaled the time—one of many through the night, I'd learn—when, if you tilted your head and took it, she'd pour liquor down your throat directly from the bottle, for free, and with the added bonus of pretending not to notice any blatant innuendo. Her job is to be hot but demure. She is a Daisy Duke lost on the Upper West Side. Or the Upper East Side, or in Midtown. Brother

Jimmy's is actually a chain, but let's not tarry over details now—quick, pay attention: I think she's about to innocently whoop.

Hot girls are one way that the restaurant, which opened in 1988 and now has six locations in Manhattan, pays homage to the natural resources of North Carolina. Others include the barbecue menu, the picnic-table and cartoon-pig decor, and a clientele so Greek that, as a support system, it rivals the most ostentatious columns in UNC's frat court.

The restaurant's sound track, on the other hand, is singularly Bro-Jim. There is nothing North Carolinian about listening to Alanis Morissette during dinner. There is no salty Tidewater myth whose final moral espouses the digestive merits of pondering the irony inherent in rain on your wedding day.

But even if a superband composed of the Connells, Ben Folds, Tori Amos, Charlie Daniels, and the ghost of Nina Simone wandered from table to table mariachi style, it wouldn't change the fact that Brother Jimmy's is one big hunk of cubic zirconia. I don't mean to disparage the place. It's fine for what it is: a Coyote Ugly–style theme restaurant. And considering that's what it is, the food is pretty good. Compared with other barbecue in New York, they're doing all right. But Brother Jimmy's doesn't compare itself to its neighbors. Instead, its website lists as inspiration one of the best barbecue restaurants in the world: Wilber's in Goldsboro, North Carolina, a nationally renowned, award-winning establishment where presidents have dined. Or at least I assume that is the establishment to which they refer; I've never heard of a famous "Wilbur's." The mention is confounding. Why even bring it up? Especially if you're going to misspell it! They were doing fine before they reminded me of something better. It would be like if Alanis Morissette tried to cover an Aretha Franklin song. And then attributed it to "Urethra."

As for the boobtastic staff, I am not impressed. A collection of the hottest waitresses in all of New York would pale in comparison to a random selection of North Carolina girls. Even Southern girls who wind up toothless and sagging on an episode of *Cops* are hotter than your girlfriend. You could pull an "after" picture of a North Carolina girl from the Faces of Meth project and Tyra Banks would say she looked fierce.

I don't care to investigate why this is true, I just know that it is; I grew up with them. Living in constant comparison with these goddesses was tough on the ego. I didn't know I was a relatively attractive person until I left Mount Olympus. Only in New York did men begin to approach me, which I found utterly perplexing: How could they know I was the "funny one" if we hadn't spoken yet?

If you want to see real hot Southern girls in New York, forget Brother Jimmy's; go to the Church Party. Every December, a group of UNC and UVA grads put together an event that started more than twenty years ago as a small Christmas party among friends and has since grown into a black-tie charity affair, which annually sells more than a thousand tickets and benefits a cancer research center. It is still attended, predominantly, by New Yorkers hailing from Virginia and the Carolinas, most of whom are in their early twenties and drink to get drunk. And it is something else I threw myself back into, after declining the invitation for many years, during my desperately-seeking-Southern period; in fact I became a host.

While standing at the dance floor's perimeter, my friend Scott introduced me to his coworker, Mark, who was attending the Church Party for the first time. He didn't talk much. He mostly sipped his lowball and stared. Scott later told me that Mark came because he'd heard how hot the girls were.

ME: Are you serious? He paid $185 for the opportu-
         nity to hit on strangers?

SCOTT: Jane, a lot of guys do. You didn't know? It
      happens every year. It's a huge selling point.

So, there you have it: Southern girls are so hot they're curing cancer.

At Brother Jimmy's, they cure hangovers. The owners claim to foster a place where Southerners in New York can go to feel at home, but how can that be true when the decorations are placed just so, and everything's a little too waxy? It feels like there's something sticky on you that you can't wash off. A glue. A glue affixed to items in a diorama.

Geez, I'm really giving it to Brother Jimmy's. It's just a barbecue joint. What's my deal? So what if it's engaged in a misguided search for an authenticity that cannot exist beyond its own borders? After all, that's exactly what I was doing. Oh, right, of course: *That's what I was doing.* Classic projection of self-loathing. Sorry, Bro.

I felt like a character in a romantic comedy who, having wronged her lover, races to the airport to apologize before he boards a plane and leaves forever. "I'm sorry, North Carolina! I'm not really dating New York, I promise. You're the one I love. Please come back!"

And that's my problem: I want it to come to me. But I can't import the South, not through pictures tacked to my walls, recipes created on my stove, or sayings inserted into my vocabulary. Because as soon as I bring those things to New York, they become part of my New York life, and are, therefore, instantly bereft of the quality I'd sought. Regions don't travel. People do.

It'd been a little over a year since my sister Tucker left SoHo for Raleigh. We talk on the phone frequently, and I visit. I had convinced myself that her move would barely affect us. But I'd only accounted for time together. Turns out, there are gradations of time apart. Before, even when I wasn't with her, I knew I could be in thirty minutes. But miles make potential energy heavy as sand. I miss having her *here*. I miss having home a half an hour away.

She brought the South to New York, the same way my parents do when they visit and insist upon making friends with every waitress, bartender, and cabbie. The last time they came up, while my dad and I were at the American Museum of Natural History, he asked me if I knew how to remember the difference between a stalagmite and a stalactite.

"No, sir."

"The one with the 'g' grows up from the ground. And the one with a 'c' comes down from the ceiling."

Blame my middle-school earth sciences teacher, but I had never even known, before seeing that exhibit, that stalagmites were formed *by* stalactites, the dripping of the latter making the former higher, so that, in effect, they grow toward each other until, occasionally, they fuse into one.

And so, I am not ashamed to say, that sometimes, in my bedroom, I put in my earphones, close my eyes, play James Taylor, and try to grow myself toward home.

"Here I sit, country fool that I am...holed up in a cave of concrete." "So close your eyes. You can close your eyes; it's all right." "And I can hear a heavenly band full of angels and they're coming to set me free." "Cause there's nothin' like the sound of sweet soul music to change a young lady's mind." "It's time for me to be stealing away. Let those rain clouds roll out on the sea; let the sun shine down on me." "Keep a weather eye to the chart on high and go home another way." "And the dog barks and the bird sings and the sap rises and the angels sigh—yeah."

There are plenty of musicians reminiscent of home, but only JT brings me closer to it. He doesn't just sing about North Carolina;

he *is* North Carolina. The thick drawl in his voice is like the humidity, slapping over certain vowels and hugging them the way a sweaty T-shirt sticks to your back. His cadence and phrasing loll unpredictably on top of a melody the way waves roll randomly over a current beneath. If I close my eyes when I hear it, I'm sitting on that dock in the Bogue Sound, pulled out by the tide.

How could I possibly have explained that to the indie rocker? He's from Michigan. Besides, who's to say he's wrong? If he doesn't know where James Taylor comes from, then the music *does* suck. It's as saccharine as triple sec. I'd rather he disparage it than open a theme restaurant in Times Square called "Fire and Rain."

All he knows about my home is what gets the most press. And I don't deny his knowledge; the South wears many faces. My grandmother used to take me to the Woolworth's in Greensboro for lunch. I sat, eating grilled-cheese sandwiches, at the same counter where civil-rights activists staged the famous 1960 sit-in, on the same stools that were later installed in the Smithsonian. I do realize that these things happened. My great-uncle, who as a candidate for governor supported desegregation, woke up once in the middle of the night to a burning cross on his front lawn.

But I only understand this side of my home in the abstract. That South isn't in my bones. The one I know is forty-person-strong Thanksgivings, and having to buy an extra book of stickers for all of the casserole dishes that came through my house when my grandmother died. It is "Shower the people you love with love."

And it's *not* fake. When my great-aunt died, her children received a phone call from a stranger who'd seen the obituary. The woman said, "I'm sorry to hear about Mrs. Preyer. I work at the Burger King, and every time she came in, she told me I was beautiful."

"My Day with the Sanchez Brothers," By Janie

"Hello?" I answered the phone.

"Franklin has something to ask you," Lou said, and passed the receiver to my nephew.

"Do you know Lyle the Crocodile?" he asked.

Aha, the title character from a popular series of children's books about a crocodile who lives with a family in an Upper East Side town house.

"Yes!" I responded excitedly. "I just saw him the other day. He is so funny."

Silence.

"Franklin? Are you there?"

"Well," he began, because he once began every sentence that way, "I don't think I believe you."

"It's true!" I said. "We laughed and laughed; he's very silly."

In fact, I felt silly, but no matter: He'd already handed the phone back to Lou and run off. "Shoot!" she exclaimed. "I had him going this morning."

"You've got a skeptic on your hands," I said, noting that he probably recognized that crocodiles can't make beds. Or maybe he did believe Lyle was real, but doubted that I, based on the way I dress, could have any friends on the Upper East Side.

Either way, at this point, the most noteworthy aspect of the call was that my sister and I reaped great humor from lying to her child. But then, about a month later, I heard a variation on the theme. On the Saturday of a weekend visit with my dear friend Lyssa, her first child, my goddaughter, announced that tomorrow she wanted to take me to the other park, the one with the bigger slide.

"Sweetie, Jane has to leave tomorrow," Lyssa said.

"Why?"

"Because she doesn't live here."

"I live in New York," I interjected.

She looked confused.

"Do you remember when Curious George goes to the big city?" Lyssa asked.

There it was again. I've been away for so long that my life is now understood in relation to children's books. This is preferable, I allow, to living somewhere with fewer points of reference. If I'd moved instead to Malaysia, my friends and family would be forced to tell their children, "You know, the place where all your toys are made." And then it would be my fault their kids didn't believe in Santa.

And anyway, my life here does resemble a kid's tale. For example, I live beside hipsters scruffy enough to belong in *Where the Wild Things Are*. I just devised a lunch out of a leftover burrito half, a frozen veggie burger without a bun, a handful of carrots dipped in mustard, and some stale crackers with jelly, which means, like *The Very Hungry Caterpillar,* I will eat anything (and everything). Also, without warrant, I retain the delusion that I can achieve my dreams.

If I had to compare my decade in New York to just one classic, though, it would be P. D. Eastman's *Are You My Mother?*, about a confused baby bird who asks everything it sees, including a dog, a cow, and a power shovel, the titular question. The day I returned from visiting Lyssa and my goddaughter, I packed everything I owned— excluding of course the dowry box in my parents' basement—and moved from my seventh New York apartment, in Greenpoint, to my eighth, in Gowanus. I can't seem to find the right nest.

This behavior is bothersome, largely because moving in New York is a major hassle, particularly when the friend-of-a-friend mover you hired, and with whom you confirmed, fails to arrive, and his phone is suddenly out of service, and the new tenant is arriving in a matter of hours. Also, by the way, you contracted debilitating tendonitis in both shoulders, so you can't lift anything heavier than a bottle of water, which is why you're already out $100 from hiring someone to help you pack. This was not the ideal time for you to move, but when a friend tipped you off to a $1,000-a-month one-bedroom, and you'd recently been asked by the local police to deliver the license-plate number of your current downstairs neighbor who was using and selling heroin, you imagined that even if opportunity did knock twice, you might not hear it over the sirens.

I'm not telling *you* what to do, but if I were in that situation, after waiting for an hour, I would purchase a box of Entenmann's brownie bites and a party-size bag of Spicy Sweet Chili Doritos, stress eat for thirty minutes, and then call the first random number I found on a "Moving?" poster taped to a streetlamp.

Five minutes later, Arnaldo Sanchez stood in my living room counting furniture. He lived in the neighborhood. He wore an Urban Express T-shirt.

"You work for them?" I asked, pointing to the logo.

"Used to," he answered, "but I'm starting my own business."

I was pretty sure he didn't have a truck.

"I wish you'd called yesterday," he continued, "because I would've had the truck, but this afternoon it's in Long Island."

Yeah, right.

"But I can handle this in my van," he said.

"A moving van?" I asked.

"A minivan," he said. "Don't worry; it'll only take two trips. What? You gotta be somewhere?"

"Yeah, but not until 8:00 p.m."

"Aw, you'll be *unpacked* by then. Two trips—guaranteed. No doubt, no doubt."

I, in fact, had serious doubts. There was a bed, a sofa, a loveseat, a dresser, a bookshelf, two desks, a vanity, five chairs, more than a dozen boxes, and as many tote bags. But he offered me a $300 flat fee (the guy who'd bailed: $550), and I can appreciate a hustle, so we shook on the deal and he told me he'd be back in fifteen with his "men."

An hour later, he arrived with one other guy, his brother, Georgie. There was definitely no truck in Long Island.

"It's not as bad as it looks," Georgie said, when he noticed me staring at his red, swollen, and wandering left eye. "I've got surgery tomorrow."

"Oh dear," I responded with concern. "Can you see?"

"Kind of," he said. "I mean, with the other one; I can't see nothin' out of this."

I reached for the brownies and stuffed one in my mouth without even microwaving it. Then, imagining they might like to stress eat too, I asked, "Y'all want one?"

"I just ate," Arnaldo replied.

"I have diabetes," Georgie said. "That's why I can't see."

OK: So a diabetic blind man would carry me and all of my belongings across Brooklyn? While I sat doing nothing—like a colonial crossing a mountain range on a sherpa's back? Well, not exactly like that; as I quickly discovered, Georgie also had a bad back.

I looked to Arnaldo: "Are you sure this is doable?" Georgie answered for him, "I'm fine!" Arnaldo shrugged his shoulders, stuck his fingers out in what was neither a peace nor victory sign, and said "two trips."

TRIP ONE OF FOUR, DEPARTURE TIME: 2:30 p.m.

On top of the van, tied with a just purchased 99-cents-store rope: two mattresses and one three-seat couch

In the driver's seat: Arnaldo

Stuffed into the console between the two front seats: me

In the bodega buying tea: Georgie

"What's taking him so long?" Arnaldo asked the steering wheel.

"Beats me," I said, and tried to straighten my neck against the felt ceiling. Another few minutes passed, and Georgie appeared with two large plastic bottles of Snapple.

"What the hell!" Arnaldo demanded.

"I was looking for the kind you like; they didn't have it," he said.

"It took you that long to pick something else?"

"I was checking all the bottles! I couldn't see!" Georgie yelped. "And you shouldn't curse in front of Jane."

So began my day with the Sanchez brothers, the younger of whom, you've likely gathered, is Georgie. Actually, they're several years apart; Arnaldo, in his late forties, is one of the first of the eleven siblings, and Georgie, early thirties, is one of the last. Georgie had recently divorced and moved back from Florida to the house on Java Street where they grew up.

We passed a fancy boutique wine shop on Franklin Street called Dandelion. "The neighborhood is really changing," Georgie said.

"Yeah," I replied, shaking my head, expecting them to bemoan the influx of twentysomething hipsters with serial-killer mustaches, who think they can put their pants on their arms and call it fashion.

"I think it's great," Arnaldo said. "Everything is so clean now; Greenpoint used to be filthy. Do you know how much my father paid for our building in the seventies?"

"Seventeen thousand dollars," Georgie said.

"Guess what somebody offered our mother earlier this year," Arnaldo taunted, turning away from the road to look at me with raised eyebrows and a half smile.

"What?" I responded.

"Guess!" he demanded.

"A million dollars!" Georgie squealed.

"A *million dollars*," Arnaldo repeated. "But you know what she said? 'No.'"

"Wow," I said, wishing the offer had been made to me. I shifted on the console, testing the neck-craned-backward position, and eventually landing on left-ear-against-ceiling.

"Georgie! Jane's not comfortable. Do something."

"What am I supposed to do?" he shot back.

"Get her that blanket! Never mind, I'll do it." Arnaldo threw his right arm behind me and pulled a comforter from the mass of chairs, bags, and boxes. It was covered in cartoon characters unidentifiable.

"Thanks," I said, taking the blanket and folding it behind my shoulders. I leaned back to rest against a box, and the console broke beneath me with an audible crunch.

"What was that?" Arnaldo asked, perturbed. I explained, and he shifted his countenance, saying, "Don't worry about it." Good thing Georgie hadn't done it.

Then we pulled onto the Brooklyn-Queens Expressway and were quickly lulled into silence. I love that about the highway. I can be in the middle of a sentence, pull onto an on-ramp, and suddenly I'm drooling: "I remember where I hid the cure for cancer! It's in the..." [on-ramp] "...bloll-dribble-blal."

Any thoughts or concerns dominating my brain disappear into the motion of wheels spinning on pavement, and my subconscious is able to step in. You know how people have big ideas in the shower? That's what the BQE is like for me: a cleansing bath (except it's filthy).

This was the most of the highway I'd ever seen on one drive. My old apartment was in the most northwestern corner of Brooklyn. If Manhattan's streets are lines of latitude, I was at Thirty-Sixth, Midtown. My new apartment is so deep into South Brooklyn that, if we're sticking to this latitudinal analogy, I'd be in the middle of the bay, halfway to Staten Island, beyond even the Statue of Liberty, which I could currently see through my window, sitting in the water, a big copper doll.

We took the Hamilton Avenue exit and drove for a few blocks

underneath the rising highway, its foundation columns growing taller and taller in the distance.

Arnaldo consulted his GPS at a stoplight next to the New York City DOT Hamilton plant. *There's my landmark,* I thought, noting the enormity of the structure, a skyscraping silo topped with an American flag the size of Rhode Island and surrounded by enough fire-engine yellow construction equipment to make my nephews' heads explode. It looks like a NASA orbital launch pad or something.

Arnaldo took a left and turned up the radio.

"What's he saying in this song?" I asked. "I keep hearing it in bodegas."

"You don't speak Spanish?" Georgie asked, shaking his head.

"Si ves algo, di algo?" I offered, parroting the subway-poster translation of "if you see something, say something."

"Um," Arnaldo began to translate lyrics, "he is saying that he wants one more chance, that he really messed it up but he wants her back, that she is his world."

"Mundo!" I exclaimed. "I heard him say that." Then the chorus kicked in, something something *"stupido."* If you were in Brooklyn in February or March of 2010, you heard this song.

Arnaldo translated again, "He says he feel stupid."

Georgie laughed.

"What?" Arnaldo asked.

"You think she didn't know that? That's the same word, Kokie."

"Kokie?" I asked. "Who's Kokie?"

"Oh, sorry," Georgie said. "That's what we call him, you know, like a nickname . . . like 'Stupido.'"

And then we parked. They both agreed that this house was much nicer than the old one, which Kokie said looked condemned. Georgie asked me to turn on the light in the hallway so he could see better, and they lugged everything inside.

When we were back on the BQE, Georgie asked Kokie for a cigarette.

"OK, but wait to smoke," Kokie said. "You'll bother Jane."

"I didn't mean for right now! I meant for later," Georgie said.

"It won't bother me," I offered.

"You sure?" Georgie asked sheepishly.

I nodded and he lit up. Kokie, who hadn't heard us, shouted, "What are you doing?!"

"She just said she didn't care!" Georgie looked at me: "Didn't you say you don't care?"

"I don't care," I confirmed.

Georgie leaned forward and said to Kokie with deep satisfaction, "See?"

"Also, for the record," I said, "it doesn't bother me if you curse."

This time Kokie looked at Georgie: "See?"

TRIP TWO OF FOUR, 4:10 p.m.

On top of the van: a floor-to-ceiling bookcase and an upholstered loveseat

Falling from the sky: rain

In the driver seat: Kokie

In the passenger seat: Georgie

In the passenger seat with him: me

"Scoot over, Georgie, you're squishing her!"

"I promise I'm fine," I said.

"You have a lot of stuff," Kokie told me. "I didn't see it all before; that's why I said two trips. I didn't see that other desk. I thought some of those boxes were the guy's moving in."

"Yeah, well, no matter," I replied.

"Janie, looks like you're spending the day with the Sanchez brothers," Georgie said and laughed.

"But we can get it in three trips," Kokie added nervously. "No doubt, no doubt. What time is your thing?"

"Eight p.m.," I said.

"*Easy,*" he assured me.

We passed the corner of Franklin and Java. "That's where they shot Doop!" Georgie exclaimed. "Right there. Remember that, Kokie?"

"That was rough."

"The Dominicans sold drugs out of that bodega—right there—on the corner. They were always at war with the South Side," Georgie explained. Then he looked at me and asked, "You know that big building we just passed, the Astral?"

"Yes, of course," I said. "A bunch of my friends live there."

"Oh, that was the worst," Kokie joined in.

"There was a different guy selling under each of those arches," Georgie explained. "You couldn't even walk down the street."

"There's a guy selling under my apartment," I said.

"Really?" asked Kokie. "Yeah, I guess there's still some of that left. It's good you're leaving. Not for nothin', but that place is scary."

Great: I'd spent three years in a building deemed frightening by a man who's seen gang warfare.

We hit traffic, a wreck at the three-way intersection of Franklin, Calyer, and Banker. Two smashed cars had been pushed into the center of the fork in the road; a plainclothes cop directed traffic.

"Shit," Kokie said. "Get down, Jane."

"What?"

"We can't have three people up here. They *love* to give tickets. Georgie, grab that blanket."

What, you've never hidden between a Puerto Rican man's lap and a blanket covered in cartoon dogs carrying balloons? The van slowed, and I heard Kokie say, "What's up, Ramone!" Ramone said something back, and then Kokie drove off, shouting behind him out the window, "Tell your mother, 'Hey'!"

I sat up. "You knew that guy?"

"Oh man," Georgie said. "Was that Ramone? He's still around?"

"Yeah. He's a cop, I guess," Kokie replied.

"I used to go sledding with that guy," Georgie recalled. He looked at me to see if I was still interested in his memories after face planting into his kneecaps. I was.

"The trash cans had aluminum lids," he continued. "When it snowed, we'd steal them for sleds. You should've seen it in the blizzard of '77; *everything* was covered. Everything was white."

Georgie said he was sad about his marriage but glad to be home. He'd missed New York. Florida didn't have seasons: "It's not right."

"Y'all have roots here," I said.

"Yeah." He nodded his head. "I guess so. What about you?"

"Enh, I'm more of a weed."

We accelerated into the expressway on-ramp.

"I can't believe you put that all on the roof," Georgie said.

"Nah, I knew it would fit," Kokie replied with confidence.

Georgie poked his head out of the window to assess our top tier. The loveseat was essentially balancing on the bookshelf, its feet strategically placed inside the shelves. Georgie refenestrated himself and said, with a face misty from rain, "I'm worried about the wind."

"What are you talking about, wind?" Kokie asked.

"If we speed up! It might blow off!" Georgie said.

"I know what I'm doing."

Now Georgie's entire torso was through the window.

```
KOKIE:    Why are you...? Get back in the car!
GEORGIE:  I think we should go slow.
KOKIE:    I'm gonna go slow.
GEORGIE:  I'm just saying...
KOKIE:    All right, already!
```

And then I was drooling again. Like one of the Astral addicts.

I wasn't concerned about the furniture getting wet or falling off; I didn't care about the boxes in the back. It's all junk other people left behind. As I've told you before, it's trash. My laptop, a box of journals, a painting my mother gave me of angels, and the green-leaf Herend dish: that's what would be in my hobo knapsack. The rest was only brought along because I had a big apartment to fill. I'll probably toss most of it whenever I eventually leave Gowanus, after I've devoured this neighborhood and sucked on locustlike to the next. I could have left it on the street if I hadn't found a mover a few hours earlier. That I can chuck it at will is its best quality. It is valuable for having no value.

Investing in permanence is discouraged when movement is the only constant in life. New Yorkers have too many worries to also bother with insuring a car, mowing a lawn, replacing a roof, and keeping a lavender upholstered loveseat dry. I mean, really, it was barely raining.

This economy of impermanence governs every transaction in city life. Even if I plan to stay in a coffee shop, I'll order my drink "to go," in case I change my mind midlatte. My favorite way to dine out is to grab an appetizer at one place and then hit somewhere else for the entrée. I can't even put down roots at a restaurant. I can't sit still.

And I have trouble making memories. No moment is more important than another unless a substantial amount of time passes between the two, but of course, in New York, that never happens. No experience is able to plant itself in my mind before the next arrives and knocks it out of the way. It's not possible to dwell, which I find attractive. However, I am forced to document my life obsessively, in notes and on film, while it's happening—at the bar, during the concert, in the moving van—because otherwise it would be as if I hadn't lived it. As if we weren't once again driving on that section of the BQE in South Brooklyn that runs along the water.

Doll sighting in the bay.

Rising highway.

Orbital launcher.

On with the lights.

Lug it all up.

TRIP THREE OF FOUR,
5:50 p.m.

On top of the van: nothing

In the back of the van: half of what was left in Greenpoint

In the front of the van: a very sullen mood

I Totally Meant to Do That

On the dashboard: Spicy Sweet Chili Doritos

On the phone: Kokie's increasingly annoyed girlfriend

"I don't think you can make your thing," Kokie said after hanging up. "Do you *have* to be there?"

"Yes. I'm writing an article about a comedian," I said. "His show is tonight, and the story's due tomorrow."

"You're a writer?" Georgie asked.

"But it's already almost six!" Kokie argued. "Where is it?"

"Oh no," Georgie squealed. "She's gonna write about us!"

"Manhattan," I answered.

"Manhattan?!" Kokie exclaimed. "No way you'll make it—no way."

Georgie pulled his fingers into air quotes and said, "'My Day with the Sanchez Brothers. By Janie.' Oh no!"

"We'll have to get the last load tomorrow morning," Kokie proclaimed.

Now it was my turn to hustle. "I know we can do it," I said. "I'll e-mail the show's host and ask him to put the comic up last. That'll buy us an hour. And I can save more time if I don't have to call a car service— why don't *you* take me into the city, and I'll throw in an extra twenty bucks? Plus tip for you both would be three hundred and sixty."

Kokie pursed his lips and shifted his eyes from side to side, adjusted his rearview mirror, sat up taller in his seat, and finally said, "OK, but we're stopping for pizza."

"What," I asked sarcastically, "those Doritos aren't enough?"

"That stuff's terrible!" Georgie said.

Diet advice from the diabetic.

Then he added, "You should really write down that title I gave you, Janie. It's good."

I didn't tell him, but I already had.

We split a pie and got back on the road, so that this time my BQE coma was also induced by carbs. Then we coasted along the section by the water and fell back into our now familiar pattern:

Doll.

Rising.

Orbit.

On.

Lug.

TRIP FOUR OF FOUR, 7:45 p.m.

In Georgie's mouth: the Doritos

Waving good-bye behind us: my two former roommates

"They seem nice," Kokie said. "You'll miss them."

"Are you kidding? She'll wake up tomorrow and be happy not to see *nobody*," Georgie said.

"It's true," I agreed.

"You can walk around naked if you like," Georgie added. "That's what I'd do."

"Well, I definitely wouldn't be able to if I had to come back here tomorrow and meet"—I pulled my fingers into air quotes—"the Sanchez Brothers."

"Oh shit, Kokie, did you hear that?"

"Yeah, she's making fun of us," Kokie said playfully.

"Janie, you'd be lucky to spend another day with the Sanchez Brothers."

"And anyway, this one ain't over," Kokie added. "We could still get a flat."

"Why do you say that!? Don't say that!" Georgie cried. "You'll jinx us."

"I'm not gonna jinx us," Kokie spat. "Would you quit with the nagging!"

"Well, if we do," Georgie persevered, "let's hope it happens in your new neighborhood, and not here."

"Oh yeah, you saw that place on Fourth Avenue?" Kokie asked.

"There's one on Third, too," Georgie answered.

"What are you talking about?" I asked.

"Tire shop," Kokie told me.

"Actually, I think I saw three on Third," Georgie continued, and then looked at me. "You didn't see them? They're all around your new place."

"Yeah, and also those churches like Henry's," Kokie said with concern. "I don't trust those storefronts. I think they want your money."

"You shouldn't say that," Georgie argued. "You don't know that. You've never been."

They continued to bicker over whether or not Henry's pastor was fleecing him, but my mind was stuck on the auto shops. Were there really that many? How had I not noticed?

Afterward, of course, I did. The following week I wandered the perimeter of my apartment's immediate area—from Seventeenth Street to Ninth Street, up Fourth Avenue and back down Third—with a pen and paper. Here's what I found.

FOURTH AVENUE

-at Prospect: M&M Corp Auto Repair

-between Prospect and Sixteenth: Prospect Auto Glass

"My Day with the Sanchez Brothers," By Janie

-at Sixteenth: Castle Car Service

-between Sixteenth and Fifteenth: N&N Brothers Auto Repair

-at Fifteenth: Strauss Discount Auto

-between Twelfth and Eleventh: Danny's Rim and Tire Shop

THIRD AVENUE

-around the corner on Ninth: Top Notch Auto Repairs Inc.

-at Ninth: Enterprise Rent-a-Car

-between Ninth and Tenth: Mexico Tire Shop

-near Eleventh: Bay Speed Collision and Repair

-at Eleventh: El Differente Auto Repair

-between Eleventh and Twelfth: Scarlino Brothers Fuel Oil Company

-at Twelfth: Masters Auto Body

-around the corner on Twelfth: Carlos Auto Repair

-at Thirteenth: Getty Full-Service gas station

-next door to that: V&H Auto Repair Corp

-around the corner on Fifteenth: New Star Auto Repair Inc.

-across Fifteenth from that: Good Guys Auto

-between Fifteenth and Sixteenth: MINHS Auto Care Center

-around the corner on Sixteenth: the Public Auto Auction, where one can "stop and save thousands" on "bank repos, off lease, seized" cars, and which is peppered with dozens of triangular flags, and topped with a supernaturally large, yellow inflatable gorilla; it's the Putt-Putt golf course of vehicular vulturing.

"Three on Third"? Actually, there are fourteen in my immediate neighborhood alone. In an area eight-short-blocks by two-long-blocks, there are twenty businesses dedicated to transience, to keeping people on the move. Um, I think I found my nest.

The only other industry with anywhere close to as much representation in Gowanus is sign making—banners, neon work, and other signs, which I am clearly no good at seeing. How daft am I? Apparently something must be the size of a NASA rocket for me to notice it. And, PS, I googled that orbital launcher–looking thing, the New York City Hamilton DOT Plant: It makes pavement for the city's roads. Pavement!

Once again, I had failed to recognize an egregiously overt metaphor. And once again I say to you: I can't make this up! I still don't believe in fate or predetermination, but these coincidences are racking up. I'm starting to wonder if coincidence is like déjà vu: Instead of paranormal shenanigans, it's just the experience of your subconscious knowing something before you do. Taking me to Gowanus was my subconscious's way of saying, "Oh, you're only happy when you're moving? See how you enjoy living in a racecar pit." As if it caught me with cigarettes and now my punishment is to smoke the whole pack.

Generally, people with wanderlust at least get to see the world. The most exotic species I've spotted is Brooklyn's indigenous yellow gorilla balloon.

As Kokie's minivan pulled onto the part of the BQE that runs along the water, I thought to myself, *Truly this is the seedy side of addiction.*

D.

R.

O.

O.

L.

TRIP TO THE COMEDY CLUB, 8:40 p.m.

In Kokie's pocket: $360

Checking her watch: me

Taking forever in the bathroom: Georgie

"What's he *doing* in there?" Kokie asked the wall.

"Beats me," I said, humming the *Jeopardy!* theme in my head. Another few minutes passed, and then Georgie appeared.

"What the hell!" Kokie demanded.

"There wasn't any soap!" Georgie yelped. "But under the sink I found some SoftScrub."

"Let's go let's go let's go!" Kokie commanded.

In the car, he consulted the GPS again, asked me for the comedy club's address.

"You want to use the GPS in Manhattan?" I asked, realizing that the Sanchez Brothers probably don't spend much time on the island, and relishing the opportunity to cash in on one of the few benefits of being a weed. "We don't need GPS," I said. "I can get us to Midtown." *Easy*. I devoured those neighborhoods years ago.

Georgie began to speak dreamily about the night's remaining few hours. "I'm gonna lie back and do *nothin'*. Maybe watch some TV. Maybe not."

Kokie, meanwhile, was anxious to meet his girlfriend, who had called several times now. "She said you must be pretty cute for me to be so helpful," he told me.

"Tell her (a) I'm paying you and (b) I have a boyfriend."

"I don't know why she gets jealous," Kokie said. "She's gorgeous."

"Yeah, so why's she always saying she's fat?" Georgie asked rhetorically. "I don't understand why women always think they're fat."

"I don't think I'm fat," I said.

"Naw, naw, you're just saying that," he replied.

"No I'm not; I really don't think I'm fat."

Georgie spun around in shock: "Are you serious?"

"Are you saying I *should* think I'm fat?"

"No no no," he backpedaled.

"I don't believe you," Kokie said suspiciously.

"Believe what you want," I taunted.

We bickered and picked some more, and then we arrived, at 9:05 p.m. There was no time to dwell on good-bye, no opportunity to make this moment any more important than whatever would follow it. So I slapped them both on their backs and said, "Today was fun. Thanks, guys."

As I crawled out of the van, Georgie said, "I gotta be honest, I didn't think we would make it."

So I put my hands on my hips, stuck my neck out far, and said with as much exaggeration as possible, "See?!"

Resurrecting
Old Yeller

Watergate was a shock. But since then no political lie has left an American surprised. Similarly, when I opened a puffy envelope from Aunt Jane and found inside another manners guide—delivered six years after the first and annotated this time in pencil—instead of saying, "Oh. My. God." I merely thought, *Yep, that makes sense.*

Sarah Tomczak's *How to Live Like a Lady* is adorned throughout with illustrations of women from periods past: a flapper holding a candlestick telephone, a corseted grande dame admiring her feathered hat, a young miss gazing dreamily upward at a pencil-thin mustache. The book betrayed its obsolescence before I'd read a word.

But read on I did, because I found the gesture adorable (beside the underlined phrase "quality cashmere," she'd scribbled "at least 4 or 6 [better] ply"), because I ultimately had learned something from the first guide, and because it arrived with the subtitle "Lessons in Life" at a time when I needed answers. On a recent Saturday, the day after my sister's birthday, while I was sitting in a coffee shop reading, I missed a call from my mother and got this voice mail.

"Well, we're all here having lunch for Tucker's birthday: Dad, me, Jane, Lucius, Lou, Marc, Franklin, Borden, Victoria, Tucker, Wes, and baby Wes. Just calling to say we miss you."

Hearing all of their names, listed like that in a row, illustrated exactly how much my family has grown. Sure, I went to the weddings and christenings—clearly, I'm aware. But I didn't truly understand. Because, when I am away from them, I don't sit and imagine them all having brunch together. Being in purgatory doesn't just mean they can't see me; I can't see them, either.

So I knew without really knowing that since I've been in New York, my immediate family has doubled in size. The bigger it gets, the smaller that I, in relation to the whole, become. That's a good thing. Like the ply count of cashmere yarn. The higher the ply, the thicker and heavier the strand. But as my family evolves into superrobust textiles, I'm the stray thread that's been picked loose from the knit, the one you either weave back in gently or yank out with one quick tug.

After almost eleven years in this city, I still live out of a suitcase, unsettled here, but unwilling to move home. I've been so consumed by this quandary, I've written a book on the subject. Even so, however, I always knew how it would end: New York. I choose New York. Or so I thought, because when it came time to turn in the first draft, I did so without a final chapter.

I didn't know how to finish this. And when I got that voice mail, I figured out why: Because, by the time I'd reached the end, my options had changed. I thought I was choosing between two geographical locations, between two ways of life. But that's not true. North Carolina isn't a lifestyle; it's my family. Or maybe it's not that the options changed, but just that I grew up enough to see them differently. Again, it's as if I knew it before I knew it.

So now I'm all confused again. Here or there—which is home? Or, rather, the true task is to discern which of the two is more of a home than the other. I'm Southern by default. But I'm also a New Yorker. Right? I love this city...don't I? Sorry. Why am I asking you? I'm all mixed up, so much so that I sought counseling from a chintzy etiquette paperback.

Because it had arrived with a North Carolina return address, and came from the self-help section, I gave it weight, combed it for clues like it was a Dead Sea Scroll. Huge mistake. *How to Live Like a Lady* might not offer bad advice, except when suggesting "weird and wonderful diet tips" as a small-talk topic, but it is grossly underqualified for the task I'd assigned it. On the list of what should be "Inside a Lady's Handbag," I found "lipstick," "small hairbrush," and "spare pair of panty hose"—seriously, who wears panty hose?—but there was no mention of which state's driver's license.

I mean, obviously. There *is* no self-help publication for my conundrum, I said to myself, and threw the flimsy manners guide onto my desk in frustration. But when it landed with a thud on top of the first draft of this manuscript, I realized I was wrong. There is a guide. *I've written a book on the subject.*

Maybe the answer is in my words. Maybe I already know it without knowing it. I only need to read between the lines, find the clues that my subconscious left behind. I'd been combing the wrong scroll. Once again, even though Aunt Jane could never have imagined this, she'd still delivered the advice I needed.

I Totally Meant to Do That is a loosely organized collection of stories from one decade in the author's life. Contained within its pages are no abusive parents, violent accidents, or horrifying sexual exploits. In fact, there is little action whatsoever. Rather, Jane Borden thinks she can tease dramatic tension from indecision, from a childish reluctance to settle down and cultivate a home. Although she should feel privileged even to have a choice, she can't focus on the bigger picture, possibly due to a substantial preoccupation with food. Muffins, french fries, mayonnaise, brownies. We get it, Ms. Borden; you like to eat. Maybe you should put cookies on the book's cover jacket.

First, however, it requires an ending; as you said, "it is cowardly to live a life without making choices." To achieve this end, try following your own advice: "search for patterns and meaning in stories that have already been written," "see allusions and draw conclusions where a writer didn't intend them to be."

"Duh: If I'm not looking at you, you can still see me."

So now, instead of arguing with Candace Simpson-Giles, Sarah Tomczak, or for that matter Jesus, I'll cross-examine myself.

"The most perfect relationship I've ever had was with a total stranger."

Wow, straight out of the gate: what a horrifying thing to say. It sounds like the title of a stalker's autobiography. Read it out loud in a deep, husky timbre. Or, better yet, use a Hannibal Lecter voice and exchange the word *relationship* for *meal*. Either way, that's not a quote; it's a cry for help.

"They'd start saying they were tired: tired of hangovers, piles of garbage, and the stench of urine, tired of screaming neighbors, and the constant rumbling of trucks in their dreams. Tired of New York. So they'd leave."

I wrote the first draft of that essay six years ago. At the time, I recognized the five nuisances in the first sentence as necessary evils. But these days, when a Midtown sidewalk suddenly becomes a man-made trash tunnel with walls stacked four bags high, when I accidentally lock eyes with a pee-smell contributor in medias res, when I'm brought to tears by secondhand verbal abuse, or when I'm startled awake—dunh-dunh-dunh—over and over—dunh—dunh-dunh—by the never-endi—dunh-dunh-dunh-dunh-dunh, the experiences leave me heavy, cranky, and in the mood to watch a bad romantic comedy. They make me tired.

And if I agree with the first sentence of the quote, then I must agree with the second, which ultimately leads to the third. Score one for the home team.

"I'd been looking for impediments in my environment, when I should have clocked the faces of people successfully avoiding those obstacles."

So I'm just following everyone else? Um, if a pedestrian jumped off the Brooklyn Bridge, would I?

"What beautiful cooperation is born from the perpetually imminent threat of death."

Another horrifying exclamation. Instead of New York or North Carolina, perhaps I should consider Kabul. Crisis is attractive because it allows the brain a singular focus, commands it to ignore every obligation in life save the avoidance of bodily harm. Therefore, it can be abused as an excuse to procrastinate. The relationship is similar to that of an addict whose only concern is the acquiring and consumption of junk. Hm. A quick word search confirms that this is the fourth time I've described myself as addicted to New York. Consider this my intervention: another point for the home team.

"No one spends that much time in a store the size of a minivan unless considering a major purchase."

No way is this not a subliminal message. I didn't mean it this way when I wrote it, but it seems so obvious now: New York is the tiny store; buying an apartment or marrying a local would be a major purchase, a commitment to the city, which I've not been considering. It's clear that I've spent too much time here and someone was trying to tell me. Add "girlfriend" to the end of the sentence, read it again, and you'll see that my subconscious is my sassy gay friend.

That's three—in a row—for the home team. At this rate, the Yankees will need a home run.

"Problem was: I'm not much of an actor."
"She pretends to shop, but she's a spy."

Exactly! I'm not even getting away with it. Approaching those lines in this new context reminded me of an incident that happened about a year and half ago. While I was shopping in one of those cheap-o wholesale purveyors in the Garment District, an employee, a man of Middle Eastern origin, approached me from behind and asked, "Can I see your face?" Startled, I turned.

"Yes," he said. "You are not from here."

"Um, no," I muttered.

Then, while continuing to pin me between the rack of shorts and the folds of his tunic, he twisted his neck and screamed to a coworker across the floor, "I told you!"

"Where are you from?" he continued.

"North Carolina," I said, trying to fidget out of his trap.

"I knew it," he said. Then he turned around again, screaming to his coworker, "I knew it! Look at her eyes: North Carolina."

My eyes? There are people with blue eyes all over the world. Maybe not in Pakistan, I guess—which brings up another question: Someone who'd traveled to Manhattan from the other side of the globe says that I'm not from here? That's how out of place I must appear.

"I was mostly a nuisance to myself."

Here, here!

"I feel no shame."

That's redundant.

"A New Yorker's home speaks volumes."

And mine is littered with furniture I found on the street—items that are "valuable for having no value," that I'm only keeping around until something better comes along. My apartment screams "commitment phobe."

My one-bedroom in Gowanus may not be a HalfFrat, but it is definitely a halfway home. The only difference between me and Ooh-Ooh-Ooh Allison from the bar on the Upper East Side is that I turned two years into eleven. Which means, unless I want to hang a Bob Marley poster on the wall and a NO FATTIES sign by the bed, I'll have to throw another point on the home team's scoreboard.

"The home team's scoreboard."

I just did it! I'm doing it right now: being terrifically daft. How do I not hear myself use the word "home" as a synonym for North Carolina? My subconscious couldn't be more conspicuous. Another word search reveals that "home" has appeared 120 times in this manuscript. That number seems high, but I guess it makes sense; you'd read *bear* as many times in a book about koalas.

In fifty-five instances, I intended for the word to signify the South. But only eighteen times was I referring to New York City. (The remaining uses were general.) In "Groundhog Weekend," I wrote, "the distinction between home and destination has disappeared." There is now incontrovertible evidence to the contrary.

"Such as the answer to the entirely warranted question, 'Where in the hell are you going?!'"

In the wrong direction, apparently.

"Inaction is still an action. Not so in New York."

That's wrong; I was wrong. I have never made a major commitment to New York: That passivity is a choice nonetheless. Which means I have made a choice.

"While the box is closed, it is impossible to determine whether or not the object inside is beautiful."

I'm tired of hiding in a box,

"It's like living in a cell. And prisoners don't get shivved in their cells."

tired of hiding in a cage,

"As night falls, I grow fearful of lying awake, lamenting a wasted day. So instead I go out in search of something to throw the hours at."

I'm just plain tired.

"*Self-actualization rarely breeds excitement.*"

Yeah, but it's self-actualization, you enormous dumbass.

"*My thumb was unmoved to gesture up or down.*"

Until now.

"*There had to be a way to have my cake and eat it too.*"

Even if that were not fundamentally impossible, when have you ever been able to keep cake around?

"*Si ves algo, di algo.*"

It's time to go home.

To clear my head, I decided to jog. I felt excited, confident in my decision and also relieved to have made it. While changing into my running clothes, I laughed, thinking about the luncheon Aunt Jane would throw for my homecoming, and the idea of belonging to supper clubs, book clubs, country clubs. Grabbing my keys, I smiled to know that soon I would live among the boobies once again, where there are no natural predators, where one can wave like a lunatic to everyone she sees, and where no one has to scream just to hear herself think. When I walked down my stairwell, the red channel markers were on the right side of the waterway, and I was returning.

Then I walked outside and instantly remembered the spell this city holds on me. I ran past a group of college-age kids shooting a film on my block: "Action!" I crossed Fourth Avenue, while a man was walking into his front garden with a large plate of pasta salad, shouting behind him, "Bring the sausage and peppers!" I turned left on Fifth and almost collided with a child on a scooter in pink corduroys singing. Two teenagers in cornrows and white sneakers stood outside the Blockbuster, bitching loudly about boys—"but you *let* him"—with their cell phones in their hands.

I ran to Ninth Street, doubled back the other way. A guy in scrubs with a backpack headed home on his afternoon commute. A small Hispanic woman tugged a cart of laundry. A couple speaking Russian pushed a stroller; the toddler inside had a mohawk. Girls with tightly slicked back ponytails of crimped hair waited in line outside of Tony's pizzeria, a car whizzed by blaring Spanish-language music, and I thought: *How can I leave this window-box life?*

New Yorkers dip in and out of each other's lives without shame or consequence. Nowhere else in the world grants such access. We show ourselves and see one another. My friend Dusty once sat across the subway aisle from a kid who was reading the last few pages of *Tales of a Fourth Grade Nothing*. It had been one of Dusty's favorite books. While watching the child, he remembered how he'd felt when he'd finished it twenty years earlier. He watched the kid close the cover, put it in his lap, look up, sigh a little, smile, and then say to his mother, "I want to start the next one."

New Yorkers participate in one another's most intimate moments, and I want to share in them all. I, as it turns out, am "the urban equivalent of Peeping Toms." My impediment is not an unwillingness to be home; it's an inability to tear myself away from here, from the eight million people with whom I want to have coffee.

But, by definition, these relationships could never be more than snippets—how can I justify choosing strangers over my family? I shouldn't "bother [my]self with what is hidden, especially not when the real prize is always in plain sight." I now have three nephews and a niece who are growing up without me, know me as the aunt who flies in and out. Lou asks Borden, "Where's Jane?" And he points his finger upward and says, "Choo-choo in the sky."

It's time to start "digging for something rather than the absence of something." It's time for me to become the Aunt Jane. I might not be able to help them with their table manners or wardrobe etiquette, but I do have advice to offer. I mean, someone's got to warn them never to eat an entire pot cookie. Other things I've learned: Don't judge a guy by his khaki pants. Always protect your groin, even when you don't see a pole. The fake wallets are usually the ones with the "real leather" tags. Never pose alone for a Polaroid. And, finally, if a fat goombah ever calls you a "bitch," you tell him your aunt Jane said he can suck it to high heaven.

I have wisdom to share, and I don't want to do so over the phone or through the mail. I know what I have to do. I'm just afraid to rip off the Band-Aid.

Then, at the corner of Fourth and Prospect avenues, my cynical, seen-it-all New York state of mind was positively blown. I fumbled with my iPhone, trying to pull up my voice-memo application in order to more precisely record the image walking toward me: a dude in a matching lime-green summer outfit, the bottom half of which closely resembled culottes. Just like the woman at my family's Fourth of July picnic. Technically, his bottoms were neither linen nor true culottes; they were baggy, long shorts. And, actually, his T-shirt was neon. Also, his hair wasn't frosted or shaped like a football helmet. But *still*.

I might not believe in fate or angels, but that doesn't preclude them from sending me a message, which is this: My life in New York has been a picnic. It was really fun, yes, but it will end, and I don't want to be around after the mayonnaise salads have gone bad. Fortunately, though, I've still got a bit of time. Because it's not over until someone reads the Declaration of Independence.

"So I struck a deal with my new home." I will leave, but not before I've had the opportunity "to script the perfect closing statement," which is, of course, this book. And when it is published, my declaration, I will give it to New York, I will read this line out loud: I love you. "I love you!" I will shout it from bridges and the tops of buildings, and "litter countless squares of innocent sidewalk with furious mutterings": I love you, I love you, I love you. But, in case the city can't hear me, those lines will also be printed in indelible ink so that long after I've left, my smile will remain.

I know this is right. It has to be true. I must close the cover, sigh, smile, and ask to start another one.

Acknowledgments

Sloan Harris, thank you for your enthusiasm when you liked something, your candor when you didn't, and your support regardless; thank you for reading, reading, reading, and making me feel worthy of being your client, whether or not that's true. Boaty Boatwright, you should have your own Fifth Avenue parade. Big thanks also to Liz Farrell, Kristyn Keene, Josh Pearl, Kevin McEleney, and Clay Ezell.

Heather Lazare, at times you knew better than I what I wanted this book to be, and at each turn you helped me improve it. Thank you for your keen insights and for pinpointing what was absent, superfluous, or all bunked-up; thank you for always answering the phone. Lots of appreciation also to Philip Patrick and Brett Valley in the beginning, and to Campbell Wharton, Justina Bachelor, Nikki Sprinkle, Kira Peikoff, Rachelle Mandik, Tina Pohlman, and Catherine Pollock throughout. Wade Lucas, cheers for the title.

Thanks, Mom, for letting me joke about your ice-cream-eating habits, Dad for suggesting I cut the joke about losing my virginity, and Aunt Jane for allowing me to write about your underwear. Thanks also to y'all plus Lou, Tucker, Lucius, and Nancy May for reading early drafts and not, as far as I know, burning them afterward. I am fortunate to have a family who puts up with me. To all of the Bordens, Lacys, and Preyers, I am grateful for a lifetime of encouragement.

Nathan, thank you for reading and offering endless suggestions.

Whether it was "this connection feels abrupt" or "you use a lot of semicolons," they were always right. Thank you for getting on my case when I needed to work and pulling me away when it was time to rest, for keeping me anchored, cooking me dinner, finding illegal recordings of *Bethenny Getting Married?* on YouTube, and writing e-mails and drawing maps when my injury wouldn't let me. I literally couldn't have done it without you.

Lucia Aniello, Paul W. Downs, Elizabeth Barr, and Lyssa Ball, I can't believe you took the time to read the entire book and offer sound advice on troubled sections, when you could have been achieving fame, putting together a magazine, or playing with your children, respectively. Thank you from the bottom of my heart.

My fellow Southerners in New York, on several occasions you let me bounce ideas off of you, pick your brains and, frequently, steal your jokes outright. And all you got in return was egg casserole and this thank-you: Susanna Hegner, Abbie and Chris Carson, Katie Kosma, Cathy and Brian Walsh, Tiffany Almy, Bartow Church, Jamie Hancock, and all of the others with whom I lamented the lack of pimiento cheese in Gristedes.

Thank you to fellow New Yorkers who gave me ideas: Alex Perry, Will Hines, Andy Secunda, Dan Powell, John Carney, and Meghan Keane; to everyone at *Time Out New York* past and present and especially Joe Angio, Michael Freidson, Ethan LaCroix, and Matthew Love; to the teachers and professors who planted in my head most of the ideas in this book: Susan Navarette, Ruel Tyson, William Peck, and Rob Seals; to John Hodgman for publishing an early essay and instilling in me the confidence to write a book; to Dan Rabinow for making an introduction; to Locke Clifford and Eric Chase (Greenwich Village Literary Pub Crawl) for confirming facts; and to Lewis Carroll, off of whom I blatantly ripped.